FICTIONS OF DISCOURSE:
READING NARRATIVE THEORY

THEORY / CULTURE

Editors: Linda Hutcheon, Gary Leonard,
Janet Paterson, and Paul Perron

PATRICK O'NEILL

Fictions of Discourse:
Reading Narrative Theory

UNIVERSITY OF TORONTO PRESS
Toronto Buffalo London

© University of Toronto Press Incorporated 1994
Toronto Buffalo London
Printed in Canada
ISBN 0-8020-0468-7

Printed on acid-free paper

Canadian Cataloguing in Publication Data

O'Neill, Patrick, 1945–
 Fictions of discourse : reading narrative theory

 (Theory/culture)
 Includes bibliographical references and index.
 ISBN 0-8020-0468-7

 1. Narration (Rhetoric). I. Title. II. Series.

 PN212.054 1994   808   C94-932010-2

University of Toronto Press acknowledges the financial assistance
to its publishing program of the Canada Council and the Ontario
Arts Council.

This book has been published with the help of a grant from the
Canadian Federation for the Humanities, using funds provided by
the Social Sciences and Humanities Research Council of Canada.

For Trudi,
who tells it like it is;

Conor, Owen, Brian, and Siobhán,
whose story continues;

and Zeno,
who told it like it wasn't.

Contents

Conclusion 155

Acknowledgments

Certain ideas first presented in my earlier book *The Comedy of Entropy: Humour, Narrative, Reading* (Toronto: University of Toronto Press, 1990) concerning the ludic or gamelike qualities of narrative as a semiotic system are here further developed, especially in chapters 1 and 5. Chapter 4, here slightly revised, first appeared as 'Points of Origin: On Focalization in Narrative,' in *Canadian Review of Comparative Literature*, 19 (1992): 331–50. The greater part of chapter 6 first appeared in print as 'Kafka across the Intertexts: On Authority in Translation,' in *Kafka pluriel: Réécriture et tradition*, ed. Monique Moser-Verrey, a special issue of *TTR – Traduction, Terminologie, Rédaction: Etudes sur le texte et ses transformations* (Montreal) 5.2 (1992): 19–40. Earlier versions of chapter 6 were delivered to audiences at McMaster University, the University of Toronto, Queen's University, Laurentian University, the University of Victoria, the University of British Columbia, and the University of Manitoba. My thanks are due to audiences at these universities for valuable feedback, as also to the participants in a Comparative Literature seminar at the University of British Columbia, where this chapter had its origin; to Barbara Sinnemann, whose MA thesis on English translations of *Das Urteil* was written at Queen's University under my direction; and to Roberta Ascarelli of the University of Toronto, who kindly provided me with Italian translations of *Das Urteil*. Former students at the University of British Columbia and Queen's University whose contributions over the years helped me eventually to formulate my ideas less incoherently include especially David Darby, Peter Gölz, and Erk Grimm. Two anonymous readers at University of Toronto Press rendered valuable assistance in eliminating (or at least alleviating) further blind spots, and those that remain are all my own work. I am grateful to Queen's University for a year of sabbatical leave during which most of the final draft was written and to the Canadian Federation for the Humanities for a grant in aid of publication.

FICTIONS OF DISCOURSE:
READING NARRATIVE THEORY

Introduction

This book is about narrative, specifically literary narrative; it is
about narratology, that branch of contemporary narrative theory
focusing specifically on the analysis of narrative structure; and it
is about the all-encompassing play of contextual and intertextual
factors that simultaneously allow and constrain us to behave the
way we do when we read (or write) either narrative (as described
by narratology) or narratology (which is itself a form of narrative). And throughout, cutting across all three of these areas of
investigation, it is about what we may call the Zeno Principle,
namely the principle that narrative as a discursive system is always potentially subversive both of the story it ostensibly reconstructs and of its own telling of that story.

The essential point of narrative, as everyone knows, is that it
tells a story. In the course of our investigation, however, we shall
discuss the implications of what one might call the inherent and
simultaneous countertendency of narrative precisely *not* to tell a
story – for narrative, by its nature, always contains the seeds of
its own subversion. The founding principle upon which contemporary narratology is constructed is that narrative is an essentially divided endeavour, involving the *what* of the story told and
the *how* of its telling – or to employ the appropriate technical
terms, involving the *story* (or narrative content) and the *discourse*
(or narrative presentation). On the one hand, the most obvious
and 'natural' function of narrative discourse is thus to be a completely transparent container for the story, to efface itself com-

pletely, to get on with it, to get the story *told*. On the other hand, and this is where our investigation finds its starting-point, narrative discourse, especially literary narrative discourse, is also expected not just to get the story *told* but to do so *interestingly* – which is to say, however, that far from effacing itself it should in fact foreground itself. The central point about narrative discourse to be considered here is that, in consequence of this division, discourse is always potentially subversive of its ostensibly 'natural' role as instrument or vehicle. The emblematic figure in this context is the pre-Socratic philosopher Zeno of Elea, who notoriously demonstrated, precisely by means of a virtuoso flaunting of the possibilities of narrative discourse, that stories we all know to be entirely possible can 'in fact' never take place – an ironic inversion of the more common practice where narrative discourse presents stories we know could never take place but 'in fact' do.

The importance of discursive play is by no means a discovery of twentieth-century post-modernism, much industrious self-advertisement on the part of twentieth-century post-modernists notwithstanding. There are good reasons, indeed, for declaring the world's first post-modernist to have been none other than Zeno, who flourished during the fifth century B.C. Born a century or so before Aristotle, and a disciple of the philosopher Parmenides of Elea, a Greek colony in southern Italy, Zeno is celebrated for the brilliant logical paradoxes with which he simultaneously defends Parmenides' doctrine of the existence of a single indivisible and immutable reality ('the one') and indulges (if somewhat anachronistically) in the first recorded attempt to *épater les bourgeois* by radically undermining the common-sense notions of plurality and motion informing 'the many,' declared by Parmenides to be illusory. Three of the most famous of Zeno's arguments are commonly known respectively as the Achilles Paradox, the Dichotomy Paradox, and the Arrow Paradox, all of which set out to deconstruct the concept of motion. In all three cases, Zeno achieves his splendidly subversive narrative effect by ensuring on the one hand that his audience will immediately anticipate a particular common-sense story as the one and only 'real' story that will adequately account for the narrative facts presented, while on the other hand demonstrating, by means of an ostentatiously eccentric mode of discursive presentation, that this 'real' story constructed by the reader is 'in fact' impossible. The hapless reader, in short, is presented with a discursive paradox that is simultaneously both demonstrably fallacious as *story* and entirely irrefutable in the terms of its own *discourse*.

In the first of these arguments Achilles, the fastest man in Greece, matches his speed ludicrously against one of the slowest of animals, a tortoise. With exemplary sportsmanship, Achilles, who is able to run, let us say, a hundred times faster than the tortoise, gives the tortoise a head start of a hundred yards. When the signal to start is duly given Achilles sprints the hundred yards while the tortoise labours a single yard. Achilles leaps the one yard while the tortoise can only lurch a further pathetic hundredth of a yard, and by the time Achilles has shot by that point too the lumbering tortoise's lead has now shrunk to no more than a thousandth of a yard. But Zeno's tortoise, like Zeno's reader, no doubt has a broad smile on his face, and the truth should be just about dawning on Achilles by this point, too, for the paradox, now evident, is that Achilles, or at any rate *Zeno*'s Achilles, however far and fast he may run, cannot possibly outrun or even ever catch up with the tortoise, however slow the latter may be. The bourgeois concept of motion clearly leaves much to be desired, common-sense practice revealing itself as wholly illusory under the scrutiny of theoretical discourse.

The Dichotomy (or Racecourse) Paradox is an even more extreme variation of the Achilles Paradox, 'demonstrating' that there is in fact no such thing as motion in the first place, since for, say, a runner to run a hundred yards of a racecourse he must first obviously cover half that distance. In order to cover even fifty yards, however, he first has to cover half of *that* distance, and in order to do even that he first needs to cover half of twenty-five yards – and so on in another eternally inexhaustible regress. Movement, however possible it may seem to the vulgar, is clearly out of the question in theoretical terms, since to cover even the smallest distance involves first covering an infinite number of even smaller distances, and a finite lifetime does not allow for the completion of an infinite number of acts. The Arrow Paradox, finally, rings the changes on the Dichotomy Paradox in demonstrating that what the philosophically untrained eye may carelessly perceive as being a speeding arrow can in fact be no such thing, since, as a little theory shows, it is really entirely stationary. For anything that occupies a space just its own size, Zeno's argument runs, is stationary. At each moment in its alleged flight an arrow does in fact occupy a space just its own size. Thus at each moment of its flight the arrow is stationary, and since what is true of each moment is true of all moments, the arrow is obviously not moving at all but in fact remains completely stationary throughout its entire apparent flight. *Quod erat demonstrandum.*

Except, of course, that all of this is absolute nonsense. *Obviously* Achilles will immediately outrun the tortoise, *obviously* a person running will indeed move from one point to another, *obviously* a moving arrow cannot also be stationary. A simple graph, for example, will unambiguously show that the line representing Achilles' run intersects at a given point with the line representing that of the tortoise. In plain words, Zeno is all too flauntedly twisting the story, flamboyantly manipulating his audience in forcing them for the duration of their reading to ignore completely the familiar and entirely everyday 'real' story involved, namely that Achilles wins, movement exists, arrows fly. In Zeno's version the *story* ('what really happened') is evidently entirely secondary to the *discourse* ('how what really happened is told') that produces it. What Zeno's readers find demanded of them, indeed, is a ruthlessly enforced adherence to a *particular* and overtly eccentric discourse, a tauntingly slanted *telling* of the story, a discourse that provocatively foregrounds its own subversive activity and completely ignores all other potential (and more reasonable) discourses of the 'same' story.

It could, of course, very well be objected at this point that our common-sense reader and the wily Zeno are simply not dealing with the same story at all, but rather with two quite different stories: in Zeno's version of events Achilles loses, in the common-sense version Achilles wins. We could, for example, certainly construct many other entirely common-sense stories in which

Achilles would also lose, all initial readerly expectations to the contrary: he could break a leg, fall down a hole, wander absent-mindedly off the course, be ambushed by an unsporting enemy, or die of a heart attack in the course of the race, and in each of these cases the tortoise would win – unless, of course, as we easily could, we had the tortoise fall victim to some unexpected calamity also (or instead). Each of our different tellings would in fact produce a different story – just as Zeno's telling does. It could also be objected that in one sense Zeno does no more than any good writer of detective fiction routinely does, setting up certain expectations on the part of his or her readers only in order to go on to show the degree to which these expectations are inadequate. What distinguishes Zeno's discourse from any one of the competing discourses suggested here, however, and makes it emblematic for the present undertaking, is the nature of the *relationship* it presents between story and discourse, the ostentatious conflict between the *what* of the story told and the *how* of its telling, the entire *unreasonableness* of Zeno's discursive procedure, the degree to which the story ('what really happened') is demonstrated to be entirely dependent on (and capable of unlimited subversion by) the narrative discourse by which it is purportedly (or ostensibly) reconstructed.

Zeno's considerable importance for the history of philosophy (and mathematics) will not be our concern here. Zeno's legacy for narrative theory, however, is precisely this demonstration of the extent to which narrative discourse is *always* potentially subversive of the story it would seem to reconstruct. Narrative discourse itself, moreover, is read by contemporary narrative theory as being by no means merely a simple matter of a single, undivided narrative voice, but rather as consisting necessarily of multiple and multiply interactive discursive levels – each of which, as we shall see, may also be read as exercising a potentially subversive influence on all of the others. Zeno's narratological legacy in the wider sense is thus what I am calling the Zeno Principle: narrative discourse is always potentially subversive both of the story it ostensibly reconstructs and of its own telling of that story. Our inheritance from Zeno is thus simultaneously a legacy of challenge and a legacy of suspicion, an emblematic reminder of the continued necessity for the *reading* of narrative discourse on the part of both writers and readers, the former perennially exploiting discourse for its ambiguities and polyvalence, the latter perennially suspecting it for its potential (indeed, as far as theory is concerned, inevitable) unreliability.

The present project sets out to examine in various contexts various aspects of this systemic ambiguity and unreliability, and thus to focus on the systemic implications of the most centrally important complex of theoretical questions concerning narrative – the nature of narrative discourse itself. Chapter 1 discusses the relationship between story and discourse on the one hand, the relationship between narrative and narratology on the other, and the essentially ludic and self-interrogative implications of each. Chapter 2 discusses some of the ways in which characters, events, and settings may be read (and written) as unstably existing across the boundary of story and discourse. Chapter 3 discusses the interplay of narrative voices in any narrative transaction and the degree to which narrative is ultimately always a form of multiply compound discourse, and chapter 4 examines the powerful discursive implications of the likewise always multiple process of focalization in narrative. Chapter 5 moves beyond the limits of traditional narratological concern to a consideration of the systemic effects of contextual and intertextual restraints, and chapter 6 develops the interrelated concepts of metatextuality and intertextuality in the specific context of literary translation, the most familiar example of a narrative discourse that is overtly doubled. While essentially working within the conceptual framework provided by the classical French narratology of the sixties and its continuators in the seventies and eighties, this book therefore ultimately attempts both to expand and to problematize the structural model of narrative proposed by this centrally important tradition of narrative theory.

While terminological excess will in principle be avoided, it will evidently none the less be frequently necessary in such a context to employ the specialized terminology of narrative theory. One reader's indispensable technical vocabulary, of course, is another reader's jargon, for jargon shares with garden weeds the property of being context-specific. Certain weeds (daisies, foxgloves, forget-me-nots) and certain items of jargon (metaphor, simile, enjambment) eventually make the interdiscursive leap to social respectability; others are condemned to permanent pariah status. Unnecessary use of jargon is properly deplored by all right-minded readers; contextually appropriate terminological usage, however, is a vital and a powerful tool, allowing us to isolate distinctions that would otherwise remain obscured or entirely invisible.

Any given terminology – indeed, any given theoretical orientation – is by the same token not only a tool that allows us to dissect and subdivide our subject-matter in certain ways, it is also and simultaneously a mould that constrains us to do so. As Werner Heisenberg long since demonstrated in the field of theoretical physics, not only do the questions we ask shape the answers we obtain, the answers we wish to obtain also shape the questions we agree to ask. Before proceeding any further, therefore, we need to examine some of the implications of the terminological apparatus we shall be using in subsequent chapters – not in the (vain) hope that that will somehow allow us to escape from Heisenberg's methodological double bind, but only so that we may the better learn to live with it and appreciate the play of its nuances. The Heisenberg Principle, after all, is essentially a twentieth-century restatement of the Zeno Principle: discourse (including theoretical discourse) at least potentially subverts the story it sets out to narrate, and thus ultimately itself also. Theory of any kind is essentially a form of narrative, relating how and why things work (and play) the way they do, and if this is true of theory in general, it is all the more interestingly so in the case of narratology, whose aim is precisely the theorizing, the *narrating* of narrative as a semiotic system.

Our investigation thus essentially concerns the implications for readerly practice of an interlinked series of interactive theoretical relationships involving three mutually constitutive pairs: story and discourse, narrative and narratology, and, ultimately, writing and reading.[1] My general intention, for what it is worth, is therefore essentially to explore some of the systemic implications of narratology as a form of theoretical discourse narrating the 'story' we call narrative. My general emphasis is thus on the relationship, the *play* of narrative and narratology, and in consequence less on attempting to provide definitive answers than on attempting to generate appropriately suggestive questions. My general aspiration, finally, is concisely expressed by Beckett's Molloy, who also worried about narrative discourse and its implications: 'What a story, God send I don't make a balls of it' (*Molloy* 77).

1

Theory Games:
Narratives and Narratologies

'The narratives of the world are numberless,' Roland Barthes begins a now famous and much quoted essay on narrative and narrative theory, his 'Introduction to the Structural Analysis of Narrative,' first published (in French) in 1966. 'Narrative is present in myth, legend, fable, tale, novella, epic, history, tragedy, drama, comedy, mime, painting ..., stained glass windows, cinema, comics, news items, conversation' (1977: 79). One might expand this already generous listing to include dreams and daydreams, jokes and advertising, psychoanalytical sessions and weather reports, professional résumés and death-bed confessions. Narratives may be variously verbal or non-verbal, true or untrue, realistic or non-realistic, fictional or non-fictional, literary or non-literary. 'Moreover,' Barthes continues, 'under this almost infinite diversity of forms, narrative is present in every age, in every place, in every society; it begins with the very history of mankind, and there nowhere is or has been a people without narrative ... Narrative is international, transhistorical, transcultural: it is simply there, like life itself' (1977: 79).

Our primary focus in the present study will be specifically literary narrative. In view of the pervasive presence of narrative structures in the way human beings make sense of the world around them, one might well expect literary forms of narrative to have always occupied a position of central importance in the literary canon. Among literary genres in the narrower sense, however, narrative, oddly enough, is very much the genre that came in from the cold. In the history of western poetics, from Aristotle to very recent times, narrative forms of literary production have traditionally been seen as very much inferior in importance to the two canonized genres of drama and poetry, which together held the centre of the literary stage for more than two millenniums, from the Greeks down to barely two centuries ago, when the reevaluation of narrative as a literary form emerged as one of the most striking characteristics of international romanticism. While the novel is now universally recognized as a major genre – indeed *the* major genre of English literature (at least) since the romantic period – this general recognition and acceptance, as Wallace Martin writes in his *Recent Theories of Narrative*, dates only from as recently as three decades ago (1986: 15).

Such previous critical and theoretical neglect of narrative as a literary form has in the interim been amply compensated for indeed, and Wallace Martin's book provides a very useful survey of the welter of competing theories that have mushroomed over the course of little more than the past two decades. The current boom in narrative theories (and in books about narrative theory) has by now reached something close to epidemic proportions. 'The recent decades of this century have seen a tremendous development of diverse theories of narrative, so many and so diverse that it makes the mind ache to think of them all,' writes Hillis Miller in not entirely comic despair in a recent handbook of critical terms for students of literature: 'Among these are Russian formalist theories of narrative; Bakhtinian, or dialogical, theories; New Critical theories; Chicago school, or neo-Aristotelian, theories; psychoanalytic theories; hermeneutic and phenomenological theories; structuralist, semiotic, and tropological theories; Marxist and sociological theories; reader-response theories; and poststructuralist and deconstructionist theories' (1990: 67). To which one could certainly add feminist theories and New Historicist theories as well. Clearly what is already true of literary theory in general after the 'theory boom' of the past twenty-five years or so is fast becoming true – assuming that it has not already become so – of narrative theory in particular, namely that intellectual control of the field as a whole increasingly exceeds the grasp of any individual practitioner.

The particular theoretical context in which the present project is situated is that of structural narratology. The term *narratology* may be used in a broad sense as a synonym for narrative theory of all theoretical persuasions; in a more restricted sense (as employed throughout this book) it refers specifically to the theory (or theories) of narrative structure. This highly influential current of modern narrative theory came to prominence in France in the 1960s and continues to flourish in France as well as (especially) in North America, Israel, and Holland. The term *narratology* itself (or, at any rate, its French original, *narratologie*) was coined by Tzvetan Todorov only in 1969 to designate a systematic study of narrative structure firmly anchored in the common intellectual tradition of the Russian and Czech formalism of the early twentieth century and the French structuralism and semiotics of the sixties.[1] There is already an overwhelming mass of specialized studies in a variety of languages on various aspects of narrative structure, written from a wide variety of theoretical orientations within the field of narratology itself. There are also several readily available general introductions to the field in English, to which, with the general reader rather than the specialist in mind, I shall most frequently refer. These include especially Gérard Genette's *Narrative Discourse: An Essay in Method* (1980, originally published in French in 1972), Seymour Chatman's *Story and Discourse: Narrative Structure in Fiction and Film* (1978), Gerald Prince's *Narratology: The Form and Functioning of Narrative* (1982), Shlomith Rimmon-Kenan's *Narrative Fiction: Contemporary Poetics* (1983), Mieke Bal's *Narratology: Introduction to the Theory of Narrative* (1985), and Michael Toolan's *Narrative: A Critical Linguistic Introduction* (1988).[2]

Narrative as seen by narratologists is an essentially divided endeavour, as already observed, involving the *what* of the story told and the *how* of its presentation. If this is true of narrative, however, it is also true of narratology, the narrative of narrative. Let us therefore turn at this point to some of the ways in which narrative is narrated by its readers, proceed then to a closer consideration of the implications of terms and terminologies, and conclude with some reflections on the self-reflexively ludic or gamelike attributes of narratives and narratologies alike.

NARRATING NARRATIVE

A naïve reader, unspoiled by the niceties of literary theory and moved to tears by the heart-rending fate of some pair of star-crossed lovers, might well regard the story told as self-evidently more important than its telling. While all narrative is a matter of both *what* and *how*, however, it is evident that in theoretical terms the fundamental of all narrative must ultimately be seen as being the telling: a narrative necessarily involves a story being *told*. Moreover, it is told *by* somebody and *for* somebody, since all stories are told to be received by some addressee, even if the teller is only talking to himself. No series of events in the real world, no matter how interesting, constitutes a story unless it is *made* to do so by a double process involving both coding and decoding, as semioticians would say, or, in more everyday language, both writing and reading. If I watch a sequence of events at a street corner, say, or in a busy restaurant at lunchtime, it is clear that these events do not constitute a narrative as they take place. If it turns out that a crime has been committed and I am asked to reconstruct the sequence of events, however, then my reconstruction both *makes* a narrative of what were originally possibly quite random and unrelated events and makes it *for* an audience of some sort, whether that audience consists of just myself or of some indefinite number of other persons. 'Telling,' in other words, is a two-sided affair: the teller tells what happened so that the audience can also tell what happened.

It will be evident from this that the audience of any narrative – the *reader*, in short – plays a highly important role in the construction of that narrative.[3] When it comes to the distinction between fictional and non-fictional narrative, for example, the reader has a starring role to play. All narrative, of course, purely *as* narrative, purely *as* a discursive system of presentation, is in principle fictional to begin with. Nothing *within* a narrative, in other words, is sufficient to allow that narrative's extratextual, referential fictionality or non-fictionality to be determined. 'The young prince eventually went mad' may refer to an invented or to a real prince; 'Nietzsche eventually went mad' may refer to the real Nietzsche or to a fictional character called Nietzsche whose life may (as in a biography) or may not (as in a novel) parallel that of the real Nietzsche – whose reality, of course, we recuperate precisely from other people's narratives, in the form of biographies, histories of philosophy, and the like. What determines fictionality or non-fictionality beyond the confines of the narrative itself is the reader's acceptance or rejection of such extranarrative descriptive or generic markers as 'novel,' 'biography,' 'autobiography,' or 'history' or contextual markers such as the appearance of the narrative on the front page rather than the comics page of a newspaper or the announcement 'This is the Nine O'Clock News' rather than 'Welcome to the Saturday Night Thriller.' The *reader*, that is to say, determines fictionality or non-fictionality on the basis of a comparison of any given narrative with what he or she has decided or has been persuaded to take as constituting the real world (which can be read as itself largely established on the basis of multiple 'narratives' – such as, for example, that of history).

The similar role of the reader in determining the literariness or otherwise of a given narrative is one that we shall return to in more detail in a later chapter. Suffice it to say here that narratives, whether received as fictional or non-fictional, may also be received as literary or non-literary as well, in a potentially infinite range of shadings. Thus avowedly fictional narratives such as novels or short stories will usually be treated as literary, while equally fictional narratives such as, say, forged memoirs will generally be regarded as non-literary; similarly, non-fictional narratives such as biographies may be regarded either as primarily 'literary' biographies or as primarily 'true' biographies. The verifiable truth or falsity of an account, however, is of less importance in determining the presence or absence of literariness than is the decision of what Stanley Fish (1980) calls an 'interpretive community' to *read* it as literary or otherwise.

In being able to *tell* whether a particular narrative is fictional or non-fictional, literary or non-literary, and that it should therefore be read in one particular way rather than another, the reader, indeed, as reader-response theory of the past few decades has made abundantly clear, becomes a second teller, a second *writer* of the narrative.[4] This, of course, is to some extent just another way of saying that both writers and readers are always already literary *theorists*. Just as the writer always either starts out with or develops in the process of writing a particular 'theory' of how and why things 'must' have happened in the particular way in which they are presented in the narrative account, so the reader always gradually has to piece together a 'theory' of how and why things turned out the way they did and not some other way. What is true of readers and writers of individual narratives is no less true of those readers and writers of narrative as a discursive system whom we call narrative theorists. Theorists are able to tell how narrative functions because they devise appropriate ways of reading narrative; in so reading, however, they also effectively write the story they then triumphantly explain. To recycle Oscar Wilde's famous quip aimed at Wordsworth: they are able to discover sermons in stones and tongues in the running brooks only because, wittingly or unwittingly, they have previously taken the trouble to hide them there.

Let us take an example. Telling what is a narrative and what is not might initially seem to be a relatively simple undertaking. One reader's narrative, however, it emerges, is by no means necessarily another reader's narrative. Our central concern here, as already noted, is with specifically literary narrative, and the term *narrative* is frequently employed among literary scholars as referring exclusively to a specific literary genre or group of genres that includes the novel, the short story, the novella, and so on – 'prose fiction,' in fact – but excludes such other literary genres as drama. Even an occasional narratologist disqualifies 'dramatic performance' as a form of narrative, 'since these events, rather than being recounted, occur directly on stage,' as Gerald Prince writes (1987: 58). While this distinction makes perfect sense as a convenient generic marker, however, narrative, beyond its specifically generic manifestations, is also and more importantly a communicative system, a mode of transmitting a particular kind of information, and here the definition of narrative certainly needs to be broad enough to include drama as one of its modes. In this context Prince's definition is entirely untenable, for the events on the stage are not merely 'occurring,' they are being *presented* as occurring, in a certain sequence, from a certain perspective, to a certain effect. That presentation, in spite of the lack of a perceptible narrative voice, necessarily presupposes a presenting instance, a consciousness that selects and orders, a narrative instance, in fact, which instead of 'telling' has chosen exclusively to 'show,' or, to be more accurate, has chosen to 'tell' the story by 'showing' it unfolding.

Whatever the experts say, of course, most of us certainly consider that we can recognize a story, a narrative, when we hear one. But what, for example, are the minimal requirements for a narrative? Theorists, expert readers, have once again differed to a surprising – and instructive – degree on this apparently fundamental question. All definitions are agreed that *events* of some sort are a central necessity if we are to speak of a narrative: '"event," or "change of state," is the key and fundamental of narrative,' as Michael Toolan puts it (1988: 14), following Vladimir Propp. (By this definition Joseph Heller's *Something Happened* might be seen as boasting the archetitle of all narrative.) But how many events do we have to have? Gérard Genette, in 1972, for example, needs only a single event: '*I walk, Pierre has come* are for me minimal forms of narrative, and inversely the *Odyssey* or the *Recherche* is only, in a certain way, an amplification ... of statements such as *Ulysses comes home to Ithaca* or *Marcel becomes a writer*' (1980: 30). Gerald Prince, however, writing in 1973, requires at least three events, linked by three different principles of organization: chronology, causality, and closure (1973: 31). By 1982 Prince is content with 'at least two' (1982: 4), and Shlomith Rimmon-Kenan, writing in 1983, is likewise happy with 'any two events, arranged in chronological order' (1983: 19). By 1987, finally, Prince, like Genette, is content with a single event (1989: 58). Prince's instructive reduction of his minimal requirements from three events to two to one, however, does not necessarily mean that he was simply wrong on both of the first two occasions, though getting steadily better. On each occasion he is able to advance excellent reasons for his particular choice, for we are dealing here with three separate readings of the situation, each of which is more or less satisfactory to the degree that the arguments supporting it are more or less convincing. Each reading is also a writing, however, for as each model includes and excludes different texts as qualifying for the status of narrative, it also shapes the concept of narrative itself.

Readings inevitably generate further readings. Challenged to do so, one can certainly see how a single event can at least *imply* a narrative. 'The king died,' for example, is a single event, but it clearly refers to two separate *states* of events, in the first of which the king was still alive and in the second of which he is no longer so. One could certainly imagine cultures where such an at first sight not very interesting narrative could have considerable force. But if this is so, what about 'The king is dead,' which does not appear to be an event at all? And is 'The king *was* dead,' even though it, too, ostensibly describes a state of affairs rather than an event, somehow more of a narrative? In the end, our answers will depend on what we think the contextual implications of the statement may be, and one qualified reader's decision may thus very well differ entirely from another's. To this extent Michael Toolan's 'minimalist definition of narrative' as 'a *perceived* sequence of non-randomly connected events' (1988: 7; emphasis added) very appropriately stresses the crucial role of the reader in deciding whether to *treat* what he or she is reading as a narrative or not.

At the other end of the theoretical scale, there can clearly be no definition of the *maximal* narrative – again precisely because of the role of the reader. For on one level, however long a story may be, it can obviously always be lengthened by the addition of further events, or episodes, or substories told by or about characters of the central narrative – a realization put to productive use not only by Scheherazade but also by Boccaccio, Chaucer, Cervantes, the baroque novel of the seventeenth century, the Victorian three-decker novel, and the television miniseries industry of our own day, to name only a few obvious examples. Even without any such physical additions, however, any narrative can be regarded as in principle infinitely extensible, as contemporary theorists of reading routinely insist. Zeno's 'proof' that no moving object can ever cover the distance from point A to point B finds a literary analogue in the concept of interpretive gaps (*Leerstellen*) advanced by such reader theorists as Wolfgang Iser. For no matter how detailed the narrative presentation may be, as Rimmon-Kenan, following Iser, observes, further questions can always be asked, further interpretive gaps can always open up: 'No tale can be told in its entirety. Indeed it is only through inevitable omissions that a story will gain its dynamism. Thus whenever the flow is interrupted and we are led off in unexpected directions, the opportunity is given to us to bring into play our own faculty for establishing connections – for filling in gaps left by the text itself' (Iser 1971: 285, quoted by Rimmon-Kenan 1983: 127). What is true of the reader of narrative texts is no less true of the theorist-reader of narrative as a communicative system, and what is true of narrative as a reading of the story presented is no less true of narratology as a reading of narrative.

NARRATIVES AND NARRATOLOGIES

The most fundamental concept of modern narratology is that of narrative 'levels.' For the most naive reader there is only one 'level' of narrative: *how* the narrative is recounted is only incidental to *what* 'actually happened.' This conflation is reflected terminologically in the fact that in everyday, non-technical language both 'narrative' and 'narration' can mean either the process of narration ('Goethe's narrative moves elegantly towards its inevitable conclusion') or its product ('*Heart of Darkness* is one of Conrad's most accomplished narratives') or both indiscriminately. The same is true of such related terms as *tale*, *story*, and *account*. The fundamental discrimination upon which all modern narratological theory is founded, however, as we have already seen, is precisely that between the two 'levels' of *story* and *discourse*, between 'what really happened' (the content of the narrative) and 'how what really happened is told' (the expression of the narrative). As Seymour Chatman economically puts it, 'In simplest terms, the story is the *what* in a narrative that is depicted, discourse the *how*' (1978: 19) – a distinction that is intuitively and immediately obvious to anyone who has ever forgotten the punchline while trying to tell a joke or recount an anecdote.

This two-level model of story and discourse draws its more immediate authority from the usage of such Russian Formalists of the 1920s as Victor Shklovsky and Boris Eichenbaum (Erlich 1981: 239–40), but has a much more venerable ancestry, going all the way back to Aristotle, who distinguishes the *logos* (the events represented, the 'story') and the *mythos* (the plot, rearrangement, or 'discourse').[5] By no means all narrative theorists are content with just these two levels of 'story' and 'discourse,' however, and several of them favour a three-level instead of a two-level model, since a three-level model allows the further distinction of the (inferred) *process* and the (actual) *product* of narrative discourse. Adherents of a two-level model, on the other hand, hold that such a distinction is either unnecessary or unworkable or both. The chosen terminology employed by individual theorists, even when they are otherwise in general agreement, also varies widely, so much so that it may be helpful at this point to present the most frequently encountered positions and preferred terminologies schematically (in chronological order) as in figure 1.1.

In the three-level model, we notice, two of the three terms take the place of a single term in the two-level system, Rimmon-Kenan's 'text' (the concrete product of narrative discourse) and 'narration' (the inferred process of narrative discourse), for example, each representing a single aspect of what Chatman is content to think of as 'discourse.' It will be evident that the same term can have a significantly or even completely different value from one theoretical system to another: Bal's 'story' corresponds

Aristotle	*logos*		*mythos*	
Shklovsky (1921/1965)	*fabula*		*sjuzhet*	
Todorov (1966)	*histoire*		*discours*	
Genette (1972)	*histoire*	*récit*		*narration*
Bal (1977)	*histoire*	*récit*		*texte narratif*
Chatman (1978)	story		discourse	
Genette (1980)	story	narrative		narrating
Prince (1982)	narrated		narrating	
Rimmon-Kenan (1983)	story	text		narration
Bal (1985)	fabula	story		text
Cohan/Shires (1988)	story		narration	
Toolan (1988)	story	text		narration

Figure 1.1 Terms and terminologies

to Rimmon-Kenan's 'text,' for example, while Bal's 'text' corresponds to Rimmon-Kenan's 'narration.' Nor, moreover, does any correspondence necessarily imply perfect equivalence, since the 'edges' of the categories as delineated by individual theorists do not necessarily coincide – even if the categories are based on the same principle of selection, which is also by no means necessarily the case. What is true of literary theory in general on the larger scale, in fact, is mirrored by narratology on the smaller scale: there are different theoretical games, played for different stakes, playing by different rules.

It is important to realize that none of these terms has any claim to unchallengeable truth, and that the 'levels' of narration they identify have no independent existence, but rather exist only metaphorically, by virtue of their interdependent *relationship* with the other postulated levels. The terms denoting them likewise derive their meaning from their relationship with the other terms of the system of which they form a part. Theory of any kind is a way of seeing things in a particular light, a way of tentatively arranging things in particular constellations in order to see what concomitant relational changes may be involved. Etymology supports this understanding of the nature and purpose of theory, including narrative theory. The Greek *theōría*, from the verb *theōréō* 'to look at,' means 'a looking at, viewing, beholding, observing; being a spectator; contemplation, reflection.' The appropriate question then becomes not whether the two-level or the three-level model is the only *right* system, but rather what the advantages and disadvantages of each as an analytical model may be. Any theoretical model will reveal certain aspects of its object of scrutiny; but any revelations it makes will always be at the cost of concealing or obscuring certain other features. It is this symbiotic relationship of what Paul de Man (1983) has felicitously called blindness and insight, indeed, that ensures the vitality of literary theory as a discipline. The advantages and disadvantages of a binary versus a ternary model can best be evaluated in terms of Ockham's razor, according to which definitions should not be multiplied beyond what is necessary. The question then becomes whether a ternary model is not only possible but *necessary*, whether the gains in sharpness of definition outweigh the increasingly cumbersome terminological apparatus. As against that, however, and still following Ockham, the next logical consideration should be whether even the ternary model is *sufficient* for our particular purposes, whatever they may be.

Our naïve reader, for example (a convenient fiction to which we shall have frequent recourse), would almost certainly see *story* as the most important of these various terms – and would be entirely as accurate as he needed to be for his particular purposes, if all he really wanted to know, say, was whether the murderer gets away with his crime or gets caught. Rimmon-Kenan (1983: 4), however, makes the crucial point for readers more aware of (or more interested in) narrative theory that the most important of the three terms of the ternary scheme *story-text-narration* is in fact necessarily *text*, since the narrative level denoted by that term, namely the words upon the page, is the only level to which we have direct as opposed to indirect access (a point we shall return to in due course). Its separate existence, its theoretically *necessary* separate existence, entirely crucial for Rimmon-Kenan's purposes, is simply swallowed up in Chatman's binary scheme, however, as we notice. We might thus well be led to ask whether there are other levels that are similarly occluded in the ternary scheme – and, as we shall see later, that is indeed the case, for neither the binary nor the ternary model is able (or designed) to take appropriate cognizance of the constitutive role in the literary transaction of the real author or that of the real reader.

In the present work we shall, in fact, stretch Ockham's patience and operate with a *four*-term model, involving the four narrative levels of *story*, *text*, *narration*, and *textuality*. The first three of these – though by no means unproblematic – correspond to Rimmon-Kenan's now widely accepted usage (which itself derives in substance from Genette), and are employed here largely because of this increasingly canonical status, in order not to contribute to an unnecessarily confusing proliferation of competing terminologies. In this scheme *story* retains the value already assigned to it in Chatman's opposition of discourse and story. We can likewise follow Rimmon-Kenan in understanding *narration* to refer to the inferred process of producing the *text*, referring specifically to the various narrative 'voices' involved in the communicative situation. If *text*, in other words,

answers the question 'How will what happens next be told?' in terms of the 'downward' arrangement of the discourse, that is to say insofar as it refers to the story of the characters, ... *narration* answers the same question in terms of the 'upward' arrangement of the discourse, that is to say insofar as it refers to the role of the narrating agent. We could rephrase our questions, in fact: story answers the question 'What happens next?'; text answers the question 'How will the account of what happens next be arranged?'; and narration answers the question 'Who is speaking?' Story is to text is to narration as what is to how is to who. (O'Neill 1990: 87)

The term *text*, however, is somewhat problematic, namely that in Rimmon-Kenan's usage it specifically denotes the *how* of the narrative, 'how the story is told,' but only to the degree that this is a product, the words upon the page rather than the process that produced them. While this is certainly an entirely defensible use of the term *text* within the terms of reference of classical structural (and structuralist) narratology, it conflicts to an unfortunate degree with the much broader post-structuralist concept of the 'text' – first brilliantly expounded by Roland Barthes in *S/Z* (1970) – as involving not just the words upon the page but also both its own process of production and its process of reception. While this posed no problem for Rimmon-Kenan within her chosen sphere of operation, since she does not consider the role of factors taken to be 'extratextual,' it does pose a potential terminological problem for the present project, which will include consideration of this dual understanding of the concept *text* – as magisterially discussed, for example, by Barthes in his essay of 1972 'From Work to Text' (1977: 155–64). In this book, we shall continue to employ the term *text* as a convenient shorthand locution in the same sense as Rimmon-Kenan, but we shall take the wider sense of how the text functions as a space for the interactive play of author and reader as the concern of our fourth narrative level, designated as that of *textuality*. In what follows, therefore, the term *text*, unless otherwise specified, should be taken as meaning a product, that which is already 'woven' (*textum*), the text as verbal artefact, as work; while the term *textuality* should be taken as referring to that 'same' text as communicative process, that which is continually *being* woven, the text as (and at) play. In other words, *text* can be taken as meaning 'the text as narrative,' *textuality* as referring to 'the narrative as text' in the Barthesean, post-structuralist sense, the text as a *possibility of meaning*, situated at the always varying intersection of authorial projection and readerly reception. *Textuality* (to which we shall devote detailed attention in chapter 5) thus answers the question 'In what communicative contexts do the *what* and the *how* and the *who* of narrative operate?' – or, more succinctly, 'How do *what* and *how* and *who* interact to produce meaning?'

To summarize, then: in what follows, we shall be using the following four terms with the following consistent meanings: (a) *story* is a series of narrated events *reconstructed* from the text, and therefore an *abstraction*; (b) *text* is a concrete and unchanging *product*, the words upon the page and nothing else, the (inferred) *result* of decisions made on the level of narration, and its primary interest for the investigator lies in its *difference* from the story; (c) *narration* is a multilevelled intratextual *process*, the (inferred) *cause* of the words upon the page, *reconstructed* (like story) from the text; (d) *textuality* is likewise a *process*, the interactive process of the text's production by an author and its reception by readers.

Textuality in the sense defined here has not been one of the concerns of classical narratology in the French tradition, whose chosen focus has been limited strictly to *intratextual* communication (e.g., between fictional narrators and their fictional addressees) as opposed to *extratextual* communication (i.e., between authors and their readers). The major advantage of its inclusion here will be to allow us (as argued in due course) to focus more attention on the essentially interactive nature of the narrative transaction as a whole, neglected to date by classical narratology. Put another way, it will allow us to consider within the general conceptual framework of narratological concerns the nature and significance not only of authorial but also of readerly (including critical) *intentionality*. This gives appropriate recognition to the demonstrable fact that while authors evidently intend their written work to have particular meanings, readers intend their own individual readings to have particular meanings, too, and the two intentions inevitably and invariably must differ to some degree. Authorial intentionality has been the preserve to date of traditional realist criticism, while readerly intentionality has been the domain of various brands of reader criticism; neither has found a place in the conceptual framework of narratology.

Whether we *need* so elaborate a scheme, of course, is determined by what we need it *for*, and we shall discuss the implications of this, too, in chapter 5. What should be made clear at this point is that the choice to work with a four-level model of narrative structure does not necessarily imply a concomitant rejection of a three-level or a two-level model. For many purposes either the ternary or even the binary model may be perfectly sufficient – and consequently, after Ockham, better. The question as to the superiority or otherwise of a binary or a ternary or even a quaternary model always depends on what we wish the model to achieve in any particular instance. Theorists using a three-level model, for example, can readily employ the term *discourse* as a perfectly satisfactory shorthand locution encompassing both *text* and *narration*, except in those cases when they specifically want to stress the distinction between the latter pair. Researchers who are more interested in story-theory (narrative grammarians like the Russian Formalists, for instance, or such successors as Greimas, Bremond, or Souriau) will certainly continue to favour a binary scheme, since a three-term scheme offers them no operating advantage, while discourse-theorists in the Genettean tradition will find themselves needing more complex categorizations for their particular purposes.[6] As always in literary theory, the principle of interactivity – the literary theorist's equivalent of Heisenberg's theory of indeterminacy in physics – is in play. To repeat: not only are the questions we wish to ask shaped by the material with which we work; the material with which we work is likewise shaped by the questions we wish to ask.

THEORY GAMES

There is clearly a sense in which all narratives are a form of semiotic game, presenting particular and particularly effective arrangements and interrelationships of real or invented events for reception and interpretation by known and/or unknown audiences. Such 'games' may occur in entirely serious contexts, as in the case of scholarly histories or biographies, newspaper accounts of disasters, police reports, elaborately wrought excuses, hysterical accusations, or convenient lies. They may also, as in the case of our specific concern here, literary narratives, occur in non-serious or 'ludic' contexts, where their function is predominantly or largely to entertain. There is certainly an evident sense in which the activity of the reader of such a narrative can be seen as a form of game, a game in which, depending on various contextual constraints, certain interpretive 'moves' are allowed and others are regarded as invalid. The same is even more clearly true of the author's activity as voluntary creator of the make-believe world of the narrative presented, he or she also enjoying certain freedoms and subject to certain constraints as regards particular 'moves.' Finally, there is clearly also a sense, as we have just seen, in which not just narrative itself but also narrative theory, the narrative of narrative, is equally a form of game, played voluntarily or involuntarily, for whatever professional or private reasons, by narrative theorists. Since the gamelike qualities of narrative theory (and literary theory in general) will play a fairly significant part in what follows, it is appropriate at this point to consider a little more closely what we mean when we talk of a game in the first place.[7]

Although it certainly plays no part in classical narratological theory, the concept of textual *ludism*, based on the contention that writing, text, and reading alike are forms of *play* activity, has become more or less a commonplace of literary criticism over the past twenty years or so, as part of the general development of post-structuralist literary theory. Textual ludism may be read as founded ultimately on a three-way distinction between *work*, *play*, and *games*, a relationship whose implications are not limited to literary texts but extend also to the domains of literary criticism and literary theory.[8] Work, as Bernard Suits puts it with exemplary brevity, is 'doing things you have to do,' while play is 'doing things for the fun of it.' Work, in other words, is instrumentally valuable, while play is intrinsically valuable: work is 'doing things we value for the sake of something else,' while play is 'doing things we value for their own sake' (Suits 1978: 15). The two categories, though opposed, are thus interdependent rather than mutually exclusive, for the same activity can obviously be classified as either work or play depending on our reasons for engaging in it. The literary critic who reads Shakespeare or Agatha Christie in order to write a scholarly article is very appropriately at work, while reading Shakespeare or Agatha Christie for relaxation is equally clearly play. Playing a game, for most people, will usually be a self-evident form of play – but for, say, a professional football player or a chess grand master, playing a game may well constitute a particularly difficult job of work.

If the categories *work* and *play* are interdependent, so, too, are the categories *play* and *game*, whose relationship is often left somewhat fuzzy even in standard dictionary definitions. My *Webster's New Collegiate Dictionary*, for example, is fairly typical in defining *game* too broadly as an 'activity engaged in for diversion or amusement; see *play*,' while defining *play* too narrowly (and in somewhat circular fashion) as 'the conduct, course, or action of a game.' The most satisfactory solution so far to this definitional problem is again provided by Suits. Quite simply, as soon as at least one constitutive *rule* is added, says Suits, play becomes game: hanging from a branch by one hand for simple amusement's sake is play; doing it to see how long you can last is a game. Games, for Suits – who coins the term *lusory* to mean 'proper to games' – are defined by four necessary conditions, namely a prelusory goal, lusory means, at least one constitutive rule, and a lusory attitude: 'To play a game is to attempt to achieve a specific state of affairs [the prelusory goal], using only means permitted by rules [the lusory means], where the rules prohibit use of more efficient in favour of less efficient means [the constitutive rules], and where the rules are accepted just because they make possible such activity [the lusory attitude]. I also offer the following simpler and so to speak, more portable version of the above: playing a game is the voluntary attempt to overcome unnecessary obstacles' (1978: 41).

Suits makes one further and, for our purposes, very useful distinction between *closed games*, where the achievement of the lusory goal (such as crossing a finishing line or mating a king) ends the game, and *open games*, whose goal is precisely not the ending but the prolongation of the game (as in games of make-believe, for example) (133–7). An open game, in other words, is 'a system of reciprocally enabling moves whose purpose is the continued operation of the game' (135). The conflict of an open game (heroes 'against' villains, say) is purely dramatic; the conflict of a closed game (tennis or bridge, for example) is genuinely competitive.

Games, as specifically focused forms of play, do not set out to discover truth. On the contrary, quite arbitrary values are ascribed to certain actions or states (and not to others). Kicking a ball under a bar as opposed to over a bar is regarded as valuable in soccer, for example, but not in rugby football, which privileges the reverse. Soccer disallows the use of hands, while rugby encourages it. In certain card games the ace is the most valuable card in a suit, in other games it is the least valuable, in yet others all cards, including the ace, are of equal value, and so on. The point here is that in all cases the privileged or 'marked' case could have been its opposite, or something entirely different, an example of what Rimmon-Kenan, quoting Benjamin Hrushovski, calls the 'reversibility of hierarchies.'[9]

Narrative theory, like all theory, can entirely appropriately be viewed as a game, whose object is the *provisional* arrangement – for particular reasons in particular contexts – of discrete data in locally or globally meaningful patterns. This, however, should certainly not be taken as in any way implying that narrative theory, or literary theory in general, is any the less important for its lusory character, or that, since it is 'merely' a game, it has no significant practical application. Literary theory is indeed a game – or more accurately a game *system*, a supergame with many subgames – but it is a game with a very considerable and complex extralusory reach.

Within the larger game system of literary theory, that form of theory devoted specifically to narrative is itself likewise a whole system of games, played by different players in different contexts for different purposes, a system in which the rules of the individual games are similar but by no means necessarily the same. To take a case in point, that particular form of narrative theory with which we have been working so far – structural narratology – is based on the foundational distinction of story and discourse. Not all narrative theory agrees with this distinction, however, or finds it equally foundational, for we can also speak of both traditional (or pre-narratological) theorists, who essentially ignore the distinction (thus radically underestimating the complexity of discourse in their conflation of author and narrator, for example, or the widespread neglect of certain aspects of focalization), and post-narratological theorists, who over the past decade or so have rejected it as an unnecessary fiction. We do not necessarily have to assume, however (though we may indeed *choose* to do so), that if one of these particular views is the 'right' one then both (or all) of the others must of necessity be 'wrong.' All three views are defensible in their own terms, but to do so essentially means at least temporarily ignoring the claims of competing positions and adopting what we might call a strategic essentialism, reading *as if* no other readings were possible, even though we know quite well that they are. To put it another way, we voluntarily agree or decide, for whatever reasons, to play a particular critical or theoretical game, operating by its own particular rules for its own particular purposes.

In these theoretical games, the particular terminology we choose (or are led) to employ is vital, just as the values we assign to different counters or pieces or moves in various games are absolutely essential to the proper functioning of the game. This value, however, is not the result of some inherent natural excellence of the item in question but is arrived at by agreement between players of the game in question over the course of time. At some stage in the history of the game of chess, for example, it was decided by the players of the game that a queen would be a more valuable piece than a pawn in the economy of the game. This value has nothing to do with the size or shape of the piece in question or the material of which it is made. If the queen is missing from a set of chessmen, agreeing to use a bottle cap or a pebble to 'be' the queen is a perfectly feasible solution. This principle of the assignability of value is a constant (even if often an unrecognized one) in all theoretical endeavour – just as it is in the very language we speak, whose essentially ludic nature has been the focus of much post-structuralist theory. As Saussure long since made us aware, the term *dog* refers to the relevant animal only because a certain group of speakers *agrees* that this will be so – while other groups will prefer (and will agree upon) other terms, like *chien* or *cane* or *Hund*. Humpty Dumpty, who clearly had the makings of a narrative theorist, saw the whole thing quite clearly in Lewis Carroll's *Through the Looking Glass* (1871):

'When *I* use a word,' Humpty Dumpty said, in rather a scornful tone, 'it means just what I choose it to mean – neither more nor less.'

'The question is,' said Alice, 'whether you *can* make words mean so many different things.'

'The question is,' said Humpty Dumpty, 'which is to be master – that's all.' (*The Annotated Alice* 269)

Ultimately, narrative and narratology, practice and theory, story and discourse, are indissolubly linked: in the end, as the once popular song puts it, you can't have one without the other. In this sense, Zeno, our pre-Aristotelian post-modernist, also has a defensible claim to being the first narratologist, in that he demonstrates the degree to which to read a narrative is always also to theorize, to attempt to explain a narrative. He also has a fundamentally conflicting claim, however, to being the first deconstructionist, to the extent that, as we have seen, he also demonstrates the degree to which reading, theory, explanation is always potentially subversive of the object of its attention. The apparent paradox here, as Borges might say, in fact conceals a real paradox. Ultimately, structuralist reconstruction and post-structuralist deconstruction, apparently irreconcilable, are only two sides of the same coin: for to explain, to structure, is also always potentially to subvert, to displace, to colonize, and explanations are always potentially more about themselves and the consistency of their own workings than about the subject-matter they ostensibly aim to clarify. If narrative discourse is inherently subversive of its story, narratology, as a narrative discourse about narrative, is inherently subversive of narrative. Narratology is ultimately about narratology, just as all theory is ultimately self-reflexive.

This does not mean, of course, that narratology or any other form of theory cannot ever be used towards non-self-reflexive ends – theoretical physics, after all, resulted in the atomic bomb and men on the moon among other entirely practical results. Applied theory belongs to the realm of work, however, while pure theory essentially belongs to the realm of play and games. The point of the game of football or tennis or golf is not that there is a single right way of playing it, that the game should ideally be played using exactly the same moves every time in order to recuperate a single unvarying 'story,' but rather that the multiplicity of available moves should be exploited to the maximum possible extent in each individual 'discoursing' of the game. The difference between *a* game and *the* game of football – the difference between the *parole* and *langue* of the game of football, to employ Saussure's terminology (1966: 13) – is that the object of *a* game (what we might call 'applied' football) is merely to win; the object of *the* game ('pure' football) is that it *be played* well. In this sense *all* games, as *langue* rather than *parole*, are thus open games – and that includes the game(s) of theory. Theory as a discourse essentially always aims to discover, or rather to invent new ways of explaining its subject-matter, more interesting ways (which, of course, means ways to make *itself* more interesting). Applied theory, as work, is primarily about its object of investigation, the 'story' to be appropriately narrated; pure theory, as play, is always about theory itself, about its own discourse. No wonder Achilles is still running.

2

Narrative Facts and Other Fictions: Story and Discourse

One of the most obvious tasks of narrative discourse is clearly to select and arrange the various events and participants constituting the story it sets out to tell. Initially this might well seem to be a relatively straightforward affair, since stories essentially amount to the doings of particular *actors* involved in various *events* at particular *times* and in particular *places*, and narrative discourse is thus merely a matter of saying who did what, and when, where, and why they did it. Different types of narrative may well privilege one or another of these elements, but most ordinary readers (or listeners or viewers) will feel themselves reasonably entitled to expect all four of them to play an at least implicit role in any narrative. Just as an apparently quite solid piece of physical matter deconstructs into a myriad of constituent elements under a powerful microscope, however, so do the comfortable certainties of such a down-to-earth view of narrative deconstruct surprisingly quickly – and somewhat disconcertingly – under the scrutiny of literary theory. Let us consider first some of the implications of the solid world of story and turn then to an examination of some of the ways in which that world is presented through the medium of narrative discourse.

THE FACTS OF THE MATTER

If somebody hits me over the head, knocks me to the ground, and makes off with my wallet, it would seem self-evident that these painful events have a considerably greater claim to priority, a greater solidity, than any mere account of them I might give, say, to the police. While this may be the case in the real world we live in, however, narrative theory is obliged to see things quite differently. The problem for narrative theory – as it will be on a more practical level for the police – is that in order to discover what really happened, it will be necessary to sift through my *account* of what happened, for, as we have seen, the world of the *story*, what 'really happened,' can be reached only through the *discourse* that presents it.

The ostensible solidity of this no-nonsense story-world of hard facts (as opposed to the mere fictions that convey those facts) becomes remarkably diaphanous the more closely we examine it, however. The apparently solid world of story, it quickly emerges, is riddled with instabilities and uncertainties. To summarize: for the external observer (the reader, for example), the world of story emerges as not only inaccessible, but always potentially fantastic, and finally indescribable; while for the (internal) actor/participant, it reveals itself as a world that is entirely provisional, fundamentally unstable, and wholly inescapable. In considering the implications of this statement, we find much to support the contention that even on its apparently simplest and most uncomplicated level, that of what 'actually happened' in a given story – whether that story is fictional or non-fictional, literary or non-literary – narrative is always and in a very central way precisely a game structure, involving its readers in a hermeneutic contest in which, even in the case of the most ostensibly solid non-fictional accounts, they are essentially and unavoidably off balance from the very start.

The same series of events, real or imagined, can clearly be presented in a multitude of different ways and in many different linguistic and communicative media. The story of the *Odyssey*, for example, can be presented in the original Greek or, in translation, in any other language; in the original poetic form or in prose; orally or in writing; on the stage, on film, or on TV; and so on. But behind all of these individual presentations or discourses there is, we assume, a single unvarying story, namely that of the wanderings of Ulysses from Troy to Ithaca. So much seems intuitively obvious. Ulysses did certain things, and later someone told the story of the things he did.

Except, of course, that Ulysses did *not* do these or any other things before they were later recounted as having happened, for, as we also know very well, Ulysses' deeds are invented in the process of telling about them. While initially it may have seemed obvious that one should logically see story as the primary plane, in other words, it quickly becomes clear that we can only ever reach that (fictional) story through the medium of its discursive presentation.

But not all narratives are concerned with events generated solely by their telling. What if the events in question – as in the case of my mugging – really *did* take place before they were presented in the form of a narrative? What about history, or biography, or autobiography? Surely here the level of story really *is* primary, while the method of presentation is surely only a matter of individual choice or skill on the part of its teller or author? Initially, the answers here, too, may seem obvious: Ulysses is an invented figure, Napoleon is not, and neither am I; and while story is therefore primary in the case of Napoleon and myself, since we are talking in both cases about events that really did take place, in the case of Ulysses, where the events are fictional, discourse is where we must begin.

This clear-cut dichotomy of fact and fiction informs much traditional writing about both fiction and non-fiction even today. The fact remains, however, that everything I know about Napoleon I have garnered from a collection of accounts told by teachers of history, written in books, presented in films, painted in pictures, and so on – *narrated*, in other words, presented as discourse, through which, once again, I must penetrate if I am to reach that true ground of 'what really happened.' Even in the case of my own very real mugging – assuming that it ever took place, of course, for my reader has absolutely no way of determining whether we are talking about fiction or non-fiction here – I will have to tell *myself* stories in order to reconstruct what must have happened: I didn't see him, so he must have been hiding in a doorway; he must have had a weapon of some sort to hit me so hard; he had disappeared by the time I got to my feet again, so he must have been young and active; and so on, in a reconstructive tradition hallowed by generations of detective stories and real police investigations alike.

The world of story, what really happened, is and must remain not only an abstraction but also essentially inaccessible to entities external to it. We can never penetrate as readers into this world. Any attempt to isolate the story from its discourse – 'War and Peace tells the story of ...' – simply results in another telling of the story. All we can ever do as readers, other than theoretically, is paraphrase, re-tell, provide another discourse. We can never invite Hamlet over for a beer, and we can never show the skeleton of the story without some tattered shreds of narrative flesh adhering to the bones.

That the world of story is inaccessible to entities other than the fictional beings who inhabit it is an entirely obvious fact – but it is one almost always ignored by casual readers and sometimes forgotten even by readers who are far from casual. Mieke Bal, for example, observes that events in the story can occur in either 'a place that actually exists (Amsterdam) or an imaginary place (C.S. Lewis' Narnia)' (1985: 7). But this is to confuse fiction and reality. The Amsterdam we encounter in the narrated world of story is in principle every bit as fictional as a Narnia or an Oz, all three of them fictional locales inhabited by fictional inhabitants – locales and inhabitants whose discursive presentation is equally subject to potential manipulation. Obviously we think of such a fictional Amsterdam as more real than a fictional Narnia – but only because we know of the existence of a homologue of the fictional Amsterdam in the real world that we inhabit. The similarity between them need not extend beyond the common name, however. Devoted North American Joyceans likewise flock to Dublin every summer to walk the streets Bloom once trod, but their ambition is essentially unfulfillable: a real entity can no more walk fictional streets than a fictional entity can walk real streets. They can walk streets with the same name, but that is a very different thing. What is true of space is equally true of time: the fictional year 1990 need have nothing at all in common with the year identified by the same name in the real world, and there is no reason, other than realist convention, why the First World War in a fictional text has to start in (the fictional year) 1914 – or start at all, for that matter.

It is to this extent that the world of story, in that it is accessible to us only through the discourse that brings it into being, always potentially exceeds the limits of the realistic, always potentially moves towards the non-realistic, the completely unexpected, the fantastic. Narrative, in fact, is arguably predicated entirely on the practice of at least potential deception, on the possibility, in other words, for the story (as discoursed) to move *away* from what really happened – or from what usually happens in the real world. Realist fiction, by its nature, can make relatively little use of this distinction between the space and time of the real world and the space and time of the fictional world. Beckett's treatment of real-world haemophilia in the at least partly realist story-world of *Watt* (1953), however, provides one good example of its effective exploitation, employed for comic ends: after a female member of the unfortunate Lynch family is described as being a 'bleeder,' a footnote blandly acknowledges that 'haemophilia is, like enlargment of the prostate, an exclusively male disorder. But not in this work' (102n).

Not all story-worlds *need* to behave as if they were homologous with our own real world, of course – examples as various as Beatrix Potter's talking rabbits or Beckett's dwellers in garbage cans spring to mind. More overtly non-realist texts and genres routinely exploit the undertow of the fantastic. Science fiction, for example, makes extensive use of it – partly, of course, because of the fact that its story-worlds are frequently situated either in a fictional future untainted by any 'actual' future already experienced in the real world or in a fictional world distant in space and/or time, 'long, long ago in a distant galaxy.' Magic realists like Gogol (*The Nose*), Kafka (*The Metamorphosis*), Günter Grass (*The Tin Drum*), García Márquez (*One Hundred Years of Solitude*), or Salman Rushdie (*Midnight's Children*) also make effective and often startling use of the possible differences between real-world and story-world conventions of space, time, and causality: Gogol's barber who finds his nose in a breakfast roll, Kafka's travelling salesman turned into a gigantic insect, García Márquez's baby born with a pig's tail. Much of the world's mythology, as well as much of all children's literature, is predicated almost entirely on the flaunted difference of story-worlds and the real world.

To the actors who inhabit it, however, the world of story *is*, in principle, real, even though it may well accommodate events that would not be accepted as real in *our* real world, such as talking rabbits, giants and ogres, princes transformed into frogs, and invaders from outer space. (What constitutes the real world is not entirely beyond dispute, of course: many people *do* believe in invaders from outer space, for example, not to mention talking rabbits.) Paradoxically, indeed, however fantastic the story may be, the story world is always entirely real for its actors; while however real the story may be for the reader, the discourse that presents it always has the potential to demonstrate that reality to be completely unreliable. What is obviously true of non-realist fiction, in short, is no less true, even if usually less obviously so, of all narrative, whether fiction or non-fiction: from the point of view of narrative theory – whatever about the laws of libel – the ritual protestation frequently posted by publishers at the beginning of narratives that 'all the characters in this novel are completely fictitious and bear no relationship to any living person' is simultaneously always both entirely true and entirely unnecessary.

Perhaps the most striking thing of all with regard to the world of story, as far as narrative theory is concerned, is that ultimately we *cannot* ever 'say what really happened,' for that world, because of its status as a narrated world, finally both evades and exceeds description. Take a very simple narrative like 'the prince slew the dragon and rescued the princess.' Here there appear to be two clearly identifiable narrative events: (1) the prince slew the dragon, and (2) the prince rescued the princess. But is 'the prince slew the dragon' really only a single 'event'? What actually happened? Did the prince creep cautiously up on it from behind and dispatch it with a single stroke of his trusty sword? Did he rush at it boldly instead and stab it several times with a small dagger? Did the battle in fact last for hours or even days before the exhausted prince finally succeeded, by one means or another, in vanquishing the monster? And so on. Similar questions might be asked of the 'rescue' of the hapless princess and what precisely that involved. And no matter how detailed our questions become, they will always leave large areas of 'what really happened' completely unexplored and undescribed.

Such questions may well seem entirely, even perversely unreasonable. The fact remains, however, that *any* event-label (such as 'A slew B' or 'A rescued B') must, to some extent, be quite arbitrary as to the amount of information it includes and excludes. 'The prince stabbed the dragon' and 'the prince choked the dragon' may both be expressed as 'the prince slew the dragon,' but they hardly describe the same event. Considering all the other methods a resourceful prince might conceivably employ in ridding the world of a dragon, the label 'slew' emerges not as accurately describing a single event but rather as gesturing more or less vaguely towards a whole family of related but more or less unspecified lethal events.

The point here is not that 'slew' is a particularly vague label, for the same holds for all event-labels, from the broadest in scope, such as 'Napoleon marched on Moscow,' to the most specific, such as 'Jim walked to the door.' The latter, for example, involves all of 'Jim decided to walk to the door,' 'Jim shifted his weight to his left foot,' 'Jim advanced his right foot,' 'Jim planted his right foot on the floor,' 'Jim shifted his weight to his right foot,' and so on, not to mention an indefinitely large number of even more minutely differentiated activities as well. Each of these, moreover, is itself, at least potentially, an entirely full-fledged event that could be absolutely vital given the appropriate narrative context: 'Jim shifted his weight to his right foot, and his startled adversary plummeted through the sudden void of the concealed trapdoor.' As Zeno demonstrated many centuries ago, there is no event so simple that it cannot be deconstructed into a potentially infinite series of *constituent* events, each certainly a part of the story, but some more obviously a *necessary* part of the story than others. (This 'necessity,' of course, is imposed on the world of story from without.)

The more closely we examine the notion of story, the apparently most basic and most solid level of the narrative, in fact, the more clearly it reveals itself as a readerly construct, a putative back-formation from what is really the most basic level, namely the narrative text itself, the words upon the page, the *account* of what happened. Story, as Rimmon-Kenan observes, is ultimately merely an abstraction from the narrative text (1983: 7). This certainly does not mean that the concept of story as opposed to discourse is any less important, however, for the story is the noumenon to the discourse's phenomenon, the signified to the discourse's signifier.

What we are calling constituent events are characterized by greater specificity and less narrative relevance than the larger events they comprise, which are characterized in their turn by lesser specificity but greater narrative relevance. As well as such constituent events, there are also what we might call *virtual* factors to be taken into account in any story, and which increase the indescribability (the entropy) of the world of story. In a narrative such as 'the prince slew the dragon and rescued the princess,' the actual *story* (ignoring the unstated constituent events) ostensibly consists only of these two actions and these three actors. But what about all the implications we may well be tempted to take for granted, such as the assumption that the prince necessarily had parents, who in turn had parents too, that the dragon presumably had abducted the princess, that the princess at some stage was born, and so on? Each narrative, in other words, produces not only a *story*, which is strictly limited, but also a largely undefined *story-world* that is in principle limitless, containing an infinity of virtual events and existents of which only the existents and events of the story proper are realized. Some narratives, of course (and some critical orientations), direct our attention more forcefully than others to this virtual world of unexplored possibilities. Critics of an older school who devoted much energy to

'Hamlet in Wittenberg, the influence of Hamlet's father on his son, the slim and young Falstaff, "the girlhood of Shakespeare's heroines," the question of "how many children had Lady Macbeth?"' (Wellek and Warren 1962: 25) diligently pursued such potential ramifications of the story world rather than the story itself – and were dismissed somewhat unceremoniously for their pains by formalist critics like Wellek and Warren. Outside of the self-imposed constraints of formalist criticism, however, there is no compelling reason at all why one should not pursue the potential development of the story-world as one legitimate line of enquiry into the world of the literary text. Indeed, ensuring that the reader does exactly that is one of the main aims of realist writing.

What, finally, of the actors who, as creatures of discourse, inhabit this world of story? Whether they realize it or not, they live in a world that is in principle the world of a laboratory rat. Their world is entirely provisional, it is fundamentally unstable, and it is wholly inescapable. The world of story is an experiment, a provisional reality under constant observation 'from above' on the part of those by whom it is discoursed. It is the world of a specimen in a display case, a prisoner in a bell jar, the world wished for by all authoritarian systems, a world whose inhabitants have no secrets – or the world of the religious believer, perennially naked before that divine experimenter's eye in the sky from which there is no hiding. The world of story is fundamentally unstable, for its entire constitution, as Mieke Bal has pointed out (1985: 149), can be changed by a single word on the part of the narrator who discourses it – the not unimportant difference (for one of the participants at least) between 'John was eventually able to outrun the angry bear' and 'John was eventually *unable* to outrun the angry bear.' And finally, the world inhabited by actors is one that in principle they cannot escape, for like Lear's flies to wanton boys, they have absolutely no recourse against the essentially arbitrary narrative decisions of the discourse – the narrative abode of those discursive gods that kill them for their sport.

QUESTIONS OF TIME

However hard and fast (or otherwise) the ostensible facts of the world of story may be, they all exist in at least one real-world dimension, namely that of time. Narrative structure is both syntagmatic (as regards the linear temporal sequence of the story) and paradigmatic (as regards the shape of the particular discourse chosen to relate the story). Nowhere has the relationship between the two been worked out more systematically than as regards the treatment of time. The distinction between story-time (*erzählte Zeit*), measured in temporal units (days, months, years) and discourse-time (*Erzählzeit*), measured in spatial units (words, lines, pages), has long been a staple concept of narrative theory. While Anglo-Saxon narrative theory has tended to concentrate on studies of character and point of view,[1] the relationship between story-time and discourse-time constitutes the essential focus of narrative theory in the classical French narratological mode, and the master text of that tradition is Gérard Genette's 'Discours du récit' in his *Figures III* (1972), translated as *Narrative Discourse* (1980), in which he establishes three basic temporal categories, *order*, *duration*, and *frequency*, answering the questions *When?*, *How long?*, and *How often?* respectively. His treatment of each of these categories, it might well be argued, is necessarily a catalogue of discursive subversion.

The category of *order* contrasts the 'real' chronological order in which the events of the story took place and the order in which they are recounted by the particular narrative discourse. Thus events occurring in the story in the order 12345 would also be recounted in the order 12345 in a completely 'neutral' discursive ordering. Genette catalogues a number of *anachronies* or deviations from this neutral mirroring of the chronological order, the most interesting of which for our purposes are those involving direction, namely backwards, as in the case of the *analepsis* (flashback), or forwards, as in the case of the *prolepsis* (flashforward). Such anachronies may be either external, involving narration of events 'before' or 'after' the main or primary narrative (e.g., 1203465, where 0 is an external analepsis and 6 an external prolepsis), or they may be internal, involving the narration of events within the main narrative time (e.g., 21354, where 1 is an internal analepsis and 5 an internal prolepsis).

The category of *duration* contrasts the amount of 'real' time elapsed in the story and the amount of discourse-time (which is to say, textual space) involved in presenting it. The unit of measurement in this category is the discursive *speed*, classified in terms of acceleration or deceleration, and here Genette elegantly proposes five canonical tempos, which he calls ellipsis, summary, scene, stretch (slow motion), and pause. The *ellipsis* is the maximum discursive speed, simply not reporting relevant events at all – or, as Genette puts it, story-time is infinitely greater than discourse-time in that the discourse-time is zero. In the *summary*, story-time is (finitely) greater than discourse-time: 'After four years at university she emerged with a passable degree,' for example, or 'Time passed, and the old man died.' In the *scene*, described by Chatman as 'the incorporation of the dramatic principle into narrative' (1978: 72), story-time and discourse-time are theoretically equal, as in the case of dialogue. In *slow motion*, a form of narrative overkill, story-time is less than discourse-time, as in slow-motion television coverage of sports events, or, say, certain parodically complete passages such as the one in Beckett's *Watt* where the combined efforts of the members of a committee to exchange significant glances with each other take six pages to describe (175–80). The *pause*, finally, is the minimum discursive speed, where, for example, more or less lengthy passages of narration of a descriptive, reflective, or essayistic nature correspond to no events at all in the story – or, as Genette puts it, story-time is infinitely less than discourse-time in that the story-time is zero.

The category of *frequency*, finally, contrasts the number of times an event 'really' happened in the story and the number of times it is narrated. Here there are four basic possibilities. *Singulative* narrative, the most normal kind, recounts once what happened once. A less often encountered subset of this, as Bal points out (1985: 77), recounts n times what happened n times, quickly tending towards a comedy of exhaustive enumeration, as once again in the case of Beckett's *Watt*, where a character sits 'quietly eating onions and peppermints turn and turn about, I mean first an onion, then a peppermint, then another onion, then another peppermint, then another onion, then another peppermint' (51), and so on for nearly half a page. *Repetitive* narrative recounts more than once what 'really' happened only once – Proust's madeleine, for example, or Snowden's death in *Catch-22*. *Iterative* narrative recounts only once what 'really' happened more than once – 'John went to school every day that week.' *Irregular* frequency, finally, occurs when what 'really' happened several times is also recounted several (but a different number of) times (Rimmon-Kenan 1983: 137; Bal 1985: 79).

These three modes of temporal presentation interact not only with each other and with non-temporal aspects of presentation (setting, characterization, focalization) but also with other modes of temporal presentation that receive less emphasis in Genette's system, such as abruptness, for example, or specificity. Contrast the abruptness with which Kafka's *The Trial* or *The Metamorphosis* opens and the expansively comfortable introduction to Stendhal's *Scarlet and Black*: 'Someone must have been telling lies about Joseph K., for without having done anything wrong he was arrested one fine morning' (*The Trial* 1), as opposed to 'The little town of Verrières is one of the prettiest in Franche-Comté. Its white houses, with their red-tiled, pointed roofs, stretch out along the side of a hill where clumps of chestnut-trees thrust sturdily upwards at each little bend. Down in the valley the river Doubs flows by, some hundreds of feet below fortifications which were built centuries ago by the Spaniards, but have long since fallen into decay,' and so on for several paragraphs (*Scarlet and Black* 23). The abruptness or otherwise with which a narrative ends can likewise generate a significant effect. As to specificity or the lack of it, the indefiniteness of an opening phrase like 'Once upon a time, in a distant land ...,' where the essential quality is distance in terms of time and space, can, by its refusal to position itself more definitely, imply a refusal also to adhere to the conventions of realist verisimilitude.

While dramatic effects can be achieved by any of these manipulations of story-time, perhaps the most striking are those effected by the *order* in which events are presented. The flashback, for example (or analepsis, in Genette's terminology), though nowadays an all too familiar irritation by virtue of its rampant overuse in tired television miniseries, is one of the very oldest devices of literary narrative. This is reflected in the notorious plunge *in medias res* of the classical epic – which by its nature necessarily involves a subsequent analeptic account of how things reached that pass. Homer's *Odyssey*, composed somewhere around 750 B.C., has Odysseus as narrator recapitulate 'the story so far' at great length over four of its twenty-four books (books 9–12), so that the reader who wished to read the events of the story in their 'actual' chronological sequence would have to read the twenty-four books (ignoring for the moment any other irregularities) in the order 9–12, 1–8, 13–24. Aeneas likewise recapitulates his adventures so far over books 2 and 3 of the *Aeneid* more than seven centuries later, once again obliging the chronologically minded reader to read Virgil's twelve books in the 'unreasonable' order 2–3, 1, 4–12. 'Unreasonable,' for although analepsis has a lengthy pedigree in narratives with consciously literary ambitions, it is relatively rare in narrative without such aspirations, where it would seem to be limited to the correction of usually inadvertent narrative omissions: 'John and I went camping last weekend. We asked Bob too, but he didn't want to come.'

Analepsis, overtly employing narrative manipulation, is a favourite device of omniscient narrators: in Balzac's *Père Goriot*, for example, it is only after we have already had some ninety pages of Goriot's fortunes laid before us that the narrator chooses to reveal the fact that 'before the Revolution Jean-Joachim Goriot had been a common workingman employed by a flour merchant' (91). Three brisk pages bring the reader up to date on the events that changed Goriot from the enterprising flour-mill employee of 'then' to the resigned old man of 'now' with whom we have already had the chance to become familiar. Prolepsis is likewise favoured by the omniscient narrator. *Père Goriot* can again serve as an example: 'He [Rastignac] realized that he was launched into the highest, most exclusive society in Paris. So that the evening held for him all the enchantment of a brilliant debut, and he was to remember it in his old age as a girl remembers the ball where she had her first successes' (152).

If there is a central narrative point to such manipulations of story-time – beyond their obvious usefulness to the narrator in achieving effects of surprise, tension, delay, and the like – it would seem to lie in their ability to establish (or, at least, to contribute to the establishment) of a particular relationship between the reader and the narrative text. In the hands of an omniscient narrator, for example, both analepsis and prolepsis function typically as devices ensuring a sense of narrative stability, reassuring the reader that everything is entirely under control as far as the telling of the story is concerned: all is already known to the narrator, and we can rest completely assured as readers that, in due course and at the most appropriate time, all will eventually be revealed to us also. If the reader has not yet had the opportunity to cultivate this sense of confidence in the narrator, however, the effect can be entirely different. Consider the brilliantly disorienting prolepsis with which Gabriel García Márquez opens *One Hundred Years of Solitude*: 'Many years later, as he faced the firing squad, Colonel Aureliano Buendía was to remember that distant afternoon when his father took him to discover ice' (11). Our immediate disorientation here – which sets the tone for the whole narrative – is due to several factors, including such thematic ones as the abrupt introduction of a firing squad and the notion of 'discovering' ice. The central factor, however, is certainly the prolepsis introduced by the first three words; which is to say, the fact that since these are precisely the opening words of the narrative, we have had no opportunity to establish a narrative 'now' to serve as an anchor for the 'many years later.' This is immediately compounded by the fact that the resultant free-floating prolepsis itself contains an at least implied analepsis (Aureliano Buendía 'was to remember that distant afternoon'), and is even further compounded by the confusing effect generated by the deictic 'that distant afternoon,' which, as far as the reader is concerned, refers in fact not to any 'distant' afternoon but rather to what emerges by the end of the sentence as the missing narrative 'now.' The cumulative effect is that we are disoriented by the sheer inappropriateness of an opening statement that flaunts our inability to provide a reliable reference point for either the narrative or the narrator.[2]

QUESTIONS OF PLACE

Discursive subversion of story by means of the manipulation of narrative space has fewer possibilities than those afforded by the treatment of time, for narrative space is clearly less amenable to discursive manipulation than is narrative time. It none the less offers a number of possibilities, since space can evidently be described in more or less detail, in a more or less orderly fashion, with more or less consistency, and with more or less emphasis on its allegorical or symbolic or ironic possibilities. Most obviously, perhaps, narrative space as setting can be used to establish a particular mood effectively and quickly, as the opening of Robert Louis Stevenson's *Kidnapped* (1886) demonstrates:

I will begin the story of my adventures with a certain morning early in the month of June, the year of grace 1751, when I took the key for the last time out of the door of my father's house. The sun began to shine upon the summit of the hills as I went down the road; and by the time I had come as far as the manse, the blackbirds were whistling in the garden lilacs, and the mist that hung around the valley in the time of the dawn was beginning to arise and die away. (9)

The rising of the sun, the newly visible mountain tops, the singing of the birds, the mist lifting from the valley, and the closed door behind him, all combine not only to establish an immediate mood of youthful optimism for the character but also to urge the reader to share it. Something like the opposite mood, the pervasive oppressiveness of much of Kafka's fictional world, is largely established by his repeated use of cramped, low, ill-lit indoor spaces. And so on. The point does not need to be laboured, for the pathetic fallacy, where the setting reflects the mood of the action or the psyche of the characters or both, has been a standard device in literary texts for several centuries, as exemplified by Lear's blasted heath, Heathcliff's Wuthering Heights, the gloomy turrets and winding staircases of the gothic, or the factories, foundries, and coal mines of the naturalist novel. The reader's reaction to the story presented can thus certainly be coloured significantly by the particular setting chosen. Such settings, moreover, once their role in the reading process has become more or less standardized, can, of course, also be used ironically, thus requiring a doubled reading, as in the gothic milieu of *Northanger Abbey*.

What one might call *prefabricated settings* are employed quite widely, seriously or ironically, in certain forms of fictional narrative: these stock props include the flowers and bowers of the pastoral, the crags and torrents of romanticism, the bars and alleys of urban realism, the prairies and badlands of the western, the vast emptiness of interstellar space, and so on. There are likewise ready-made and more or less interchangeable topoi that can be found in a wide range of fictional narratives: the desert isle (*Robinson Crusoe*), the snowy peak (*The Magic Mountain*), the indomitable jungle (*Heart of Darkness*), the raging sea (*David Copperfield*). Ready-made props include windows (*The Trial*, Joyce's *Dubliners*, many Eichendorff narratives), bridges (*The Trial* again), and more recently, bicycles (*Molloy*, Flann O'Brien's *The Third Policeman*, Robbe-Grillet's *The Voyeur*).

The James Bond movies provide a striking example of narratives that work very largely with permutations of prefabricated settings and situations and even characters: the mechanical wizardry of Q's inventions, the sexual gymnastics of Bond's increasingly outlandish female opponents, the assorted power complexes of his increasingly outlandish 'mad scientist' opponents, his own increasingly implausible sang-froid in the face of all odds, the obligatory James-gets-girl ending. In extreme formula fiction of this kind, there is a sense in which *everything*, including Bond himself, becomes the *setting* for a single ritually repeated story: handsome hero, against impossible odds, defeats villain, saves society, and wins *en passant* a whole collection of desirable female trophies – or in other words, hero slays dragon, saves kingdom, wins princess. This single story is continually retold with interchangeable personnel, scenery, and plots. In this context, it is entirely appropriate that the cinematic character James Bond has been played by a whole series of interchangeable actors (Sean Connery, Roger Moore, Timothy Dalton, George Lazenby).

QUESTIONS OF CHARACTER

The multifarious ways in which characters emerge from the words on the page, in which story-world actors acquire a personality, is one of the most fascinating and least systematically explored aspects of narrative theory and narrative practice. We shall limit ourselves here to some of the ways in which the process of characterization most obviously reflects the potential subversion of story by discourse.

The so-called process of characterization actually involves three intersecting processes: a process of construction by the author, a process of reconstruction by the reader, and, pre-shaping both of these, a process of *pre*-construction by contextual constraints and expectations, whether adhered to or rejected, such as that 'heroes' should be tall, dark, and handsome, 'detectives' should be clever, and the 'boy' should meet the 'girl' and live happily ever after. Our reconstructive activity as readers is also a complex procedure, working both from present details to absent wholes (as we progress in linear fashion from word to word of the text we are reading) and simultaneously from already fuzzily preconceived wholes which we silently modify as necessary as the details become available. We also attempt to construct characters who are reasonably consistent (who should not be simultaneously fat and skinny, or young and old, for example), and we instinctively expect characters to be roughly like real people (even if they are robots or rabbits) and grant a concomitant importance to questions of development, cause and effect, and so on.

The primary fuel for our readerly reconstruction is the authorial construction we encounter through the words on the page, and here there are two basic types of textual indicators of character, namely, direct definition and indirect presentation. The former is essentially diegetic, in that we are told what a character is like; the latter is essentially mimetic, in that we are shown what the character is like (Rimmon-Kenan 1983: 59). Both telling (*diegesis*) and showing (*mimesis*) depend on the reliability of their source, however, and it is thus preferable to think of characterization as always a matter of presentation (whether diegetic or mimetic) rather than definition.[3]

Some characters have their character thrust upon them in no uncertain terms. Mr Bounderby in Dickens' *Hard Times* (1854) is a notable example:

He was a rich man: banker, merchant, manufacturer, and what not. A big, loud man, with a stare, and a metallic laugh. A man made out of a coarse material, which seemed to have been stretched to make so much of him. A man with a great puffed head and forehead, swelled veins in his temples, and such a strained skin to his face that it seemed to hold his eyes open, and lift his eyebrows up. A man with a pervading appearance on him of being inflated like a balloon, and ready to start. A man who could never sufficiently vaunt himself a self-made man. A man who was always proclaiming, through that brassy speaking-trumpet of a voice of his, his old ignorance and his old poverty. A man who was the Bully of humility. (23–4)

Likewise Mrs Gradgrind, also in *Hard Times*:

a little, thin, white, pink-eyed bundle of shawls, of surpassing feebleness, mental and bodily; who was always taking physic without any effect, and who, whenever she showed a symptom of coming to life, was invariably stunned by some weighty piece of fact tumbling on her. (24)

Indirect presentation operates by showing characters engaged in action – or *not* engaged in action when they might reasonably be expected to do something, as in the case of Hamlet, for example, or the marked failure of Kafka's Gregor Samsa to be at all horrified at his transfiguration into a monstrous insect in *The*

Metamorphosis. What a character says, how he or she says it, and in what context he or she speaks can be a particularly effective and economical way of characterizing not only the speaking characters, but also those spoken to, and those spoken about. Characters' external appearance can be used in at least suggestive evidence for or against them, whether these factors are within the character's control (slovenly dress, for example) or beyond them (old and ugly, or prone to fiery temper as allegedly displayed by red hair). Finally, a character can be effectively contrasted with another character used as a systematic foil, as in the case of Don Quixote and Sancho Panza, Faust and Mephistopheles, Sherlock Holmes and Dr Watson, or Hercule Poirot and Captain Hastings.

Two striking examples of the reach of such indirect characterization may be found in Emily Brontë's *Wuthering Heights* (1847) and Günter Grass's *Cat and Mouse* (1961) respectively. Mr Lockwood, the first-person narrator of *Wuthering Heights*, effectively if completely unconsciously characterizes himself as a cultivated weakling by virtue of the contrast with the savagely powerful Heathcliff whose doings he both narrates and hears narrated by others. Pilenz, the first-person narrator of *Cat and Mouse*, compellingly characterizes himself as somebody who wishes to avoid the truth in his account of the life and death of his one-time friend, Joachim Mahlke. In Pilenz's case, however, the reader will find it difficult to say definitely just how directly or indirectly Pilenz is characterized. Pilenz may be characterizing himself unconsciously and indirectly, or again, his self-characterization may be quite conscious and direct, driven by a powerful feeling of guilt because of his (equally unspecified) involvement in Mahlke's death.

Directness and indirectness of presentation are relative, of course: there is, after all, no particular reason why Bounderby's metallic laugh or Mrs Gradgrind's bundle of shawls should correspond to any particular character traits, just as there is no (nondiscursive) reason why their names should characterize them. One of the most brutally direct ways of conveying a shorthand characterization – similar in kind to characterization by appearance, as in the case of Mr Bounderby – is by means of what the

Germans call *sprechende Namen*, 'speaking names,' again one of the oldest tricks of the narrative trade, going back at least to Aristophanes' heroine Lysistrata, 'she who disbands the army.' It is also one of the most obvious ways in which narrative discourse privileges itself at the expense of the story it tells. Such names – Fielding's Thwackum, Mrs Malaprop, Sir Benjamin Backbite, Thackeray's Mr Fillgrave, Mr Stickatit, Mr Quiverful and his fourteen children – are an ostentatious indication of the priority of discourse over story: what is primarily important is the narrative point being made, not the process of characterization. This kind of analogical characterization, as Rimmon-Kenan notes, 'is a purely textual link, independent of story-causality' (1983: 67). The same is essentially true of any stock character, such as the *miles gloriosus*, the penny-pinching Scot, or the buffoonish Irishman. All are characters *manqués*, limited entirely unrealistically to a single function or a highly restricted set of functions, close kin to the one-dimensional cartoon characters of modern-day television, the Bugs Bunnys, Goofys, and Daffy Ducks.

Such names can be satirically summarizing (Gradgrind), allegorically instructive (Pilgrim's progress) or simply outrageous (Pynchon's Manny di Presso and Genghis Cohen in *The Crying of Lot 49*, Heller's General Scheisskopf in *Catch-22*), but in all cases they make the point that the story is entirely secondary to its discourse. What, if any, freedom of action do the Sir Toby Belches and Mrs Malaprops and Lydia Languishes have? It is entirely unlikely, after all, that a character called Gradgrind or McChoakumchild or Bounderby is going to be the hero of a story, or even a reasonably sympathetic person. While we are quite prepared to accept this kind of guarantee that *nomen est omen* in a certain kind of fiction, of course, we would be astonished if the same kind of relationship held true in real life – or, indeed, in other kinds of fiction. We may, however, compare the common tendency to give derogatory nicknames to those we dislike (Old Sourpuss, Mr Holier-Than-Thou), especially to large groups we dislike or fear, as evidenced in the rich vocabulary of racial slurs available in popular usage.

A counterpart of names like Gradgrind, which refer to the primacy of discourse over story, are names that refer reflexively to the discourse itself. Such names can refer either overtly or obliquely to the presence of the author as constructor, as with Kafka's Joseph K. or Nabokov's anagrammatic Vivian Darkbloom in *Lolita*; they can playfully self-destruct, as in the masculine/feminine, black/white play of Nabokov's Dr Blanche Schwarzmann, also in *Lolita*; or mirror their own provisionality, like the pseudonymous Humbert Humbert, who also claims to have toyed with the idea of calling himself Otto Otto, Mesmer Mesmer, or Lambert Lambert (*Lolita* 280).

QUESTIONS OF INTERACTION

Times, places, and characters interact in a complex fashion in the narrative transaction. Narrative events are clearly a function primarily of time, setting primarily of place, and characters of both time and place. To put it another way, narrative events operate (primarily) on the syntagmatic axis, setting operates (primarily) on the paradigmatic axis, while characters are always a combination of both paradigmatic and syntagmatic traits.

This should be thought of as a matter of relationships, a system of emphases rather than absolutes, however: events can never be wholly free of the demands of place, any more than setting can ever be wholly free of the effects of time ('The trees were losing their leaves'). Moreover, very flat, one-dimensional characters can approach very close to either the axis of space – crowd scenes, for example, or walk-on roles of any kind, where characters function less as characters than as setting – or the axis of time – as in the case of the picaresque hero, who functions typically as a structural peg on which to hang a potentially endless succession of events.

Narrative space, like actors, can readily acquire a particular *character*. Thus Coketown in Dickens's *Hard Times*:

It was a town of red brick, or of brick that would have been red if the smoke and ashes had allowed it; but as matters stood it was a town of unnatural red and black like the painted face of a savage. It was a town of machinery and tall chimneys, out of which interminable serpents of smoke trailed themselves forever and ever, and never got uncoiled. It had a black canal in it, and a river that ran purple with ill-smelling dye, and vast piles of building full of windows where there was a rattling and a trembling all day long, and where the piston of the steam-engine worked monotonously up and down like the head of an elephant in a state of melancholy madness. It contained several large streets all very like one another, and many small streets still more like one another, inhabited by people equally like one another, who all went in and out at the same hours, with the same sound upon the same pavements, to do the same work, and to whom every day was the same as yesterday and tomorrow, and every year the counterpart of the last and the next. (30–1)

As in the case of actors, places can thus clearly acquire their character by direct presentation, for the characterization of Coketown is not different in any essential way from that of, say, Mr Bounderby and Mrs Gradgrind in the same novel. Like characters, too, places can acquire their character by indirect presentation, as in the case of Joyce's Dublin, Proust's Paris, Döblin's Berlin, or Dostoevsky's St Petersburg. Time can likewise acquire a character by direct definition, as in the case of *A Tale of Two Cities*: 'It was the best of times, it was the worst of times ...' (13). Time can also characterize itself indirectly through the actors who populate a particular era: the actions of the almost six hundred characters in Tolstoy's *War and Peace*, for example, present a vivid but indirect picture of the first decade of the nineteenth century in Russia. It seems evident that the characterization of both time and space, when conveyed indirectly rather than directly, is particularly apt to involve very large groups of actors. At the same time, it is also possible to present such characterization through very sharply focused central figures – Dostoevsky's Raskolnikov, Proust's Marcel, Joyce's Bloom, Döblin's Biberkopf.

SITUATING THE DISCOURSE

Narrative discourse, however, not only arranges the events and existents[4] of the story it tells, it also always arranges, sometimes more overtly and sometimes less so, the manner in which its reader will react. Genre constraints, for example, set up certain expectations on the part of readers. Thus, in the most general terms, we obviously know without being specifically told that we are expected to read a fairy tale in quite a different way than, say, a volume of Proust or a history of the Second World War. More specifically, we may draw a comparison between story setting (the physical setting in or against which the events of the story take place) and *discourse setting* (the textual setting in which the discourse self-referentially places itself). Thus the *Iliad*, which opens: 'Sing, goddess, the anger of Peleus' son Achilleus / and its devastation, which put pains thousandfold upon the Achaians ...' (59). Likewise the *Odyssey*: 'Tell me, Muse, of the man of many ways, who was driven / far journeys, after he had sacked Troy's sacred citadels' (27). And the *Aeneid*: 'I sing of warfare and a man at war' (3). Duly forewarned to expect an epic poem, the reader obediently prepares to react appropriately.

Modern literary narratives are as likely (or more likely) to exploit instead the lack of appropriateness in discourse setting. Thus Thomas Mann makes masterly use of the discrepancy between discourse setting and the story related in *Death in Venice*, where Aschenbach's accelerating physical and moral decline is narrated in a discursive style that becomes increasingly classical in its intertextual references. Joyce achieves comic effects in many passages of *Ulysses* by a similar incongruous juxtaposition, notably in the 'Cyclops' episode, where Bloom makes a hurried escape from a Dublin pub, narrowly missed by a biscuit box hurled after him by the irate and anonymous Citizen: 'And they beheld Him even Him, ben Bloom Elijah, amid clouds of angels ascend to the glory of the brightness at an angle of fortyfive degrees over Donohoe's in Little Green street like a shot off a shovel' (283).

Such self-reflexive discourse setting is not at all limited to literary usage, it may be observed. Television newsreaders regularly open their narratives with a discourse setting formula such as 'This is the "Nine O'Clock News."' Discourse setting is also frequently found in the formulaic beginning of certain classes of jokes: 'A priest, a rabbi, and an atheist were playing golf ...,' for example, or 'Guy walks into a bar, sees this horse ordering a martini ...,' or even the hoary 'Have you heard the one about ...' Many folk-songs likewise establish the discourse setting by an appropriate formula like 'Come and listen to my story,' or 'All in the merry month of May,' which economically establishes both story setting and discourse setting. Literary discourse is much more likely to treat discourse setting reflexively, however, and one important aspect of literary discourse setting is therefore typically the establishing of focalization, to which we shall return in a later chapter but which may be characterized at this point as the sense conveyed by the text as to where the narrative voice is coming from.[5]

DISCOURSE AS STORY

The transformation of actors, place, and story-time into characters, setting, and discourse-time is evidently always at least potentially subversive. One of the most flamboyant – and most amusing – examples of the ostentatious arrangement and rearrangement of a story by 'its' discourse is Raymond Queneau's virtuoso *Exercises in Style* (1947), which tells a single story in no less than ninety-nine different versions, employing ninety-nine different narrative styles to increasingly hilarious effect. The story is very brief and very banal: a young man on a crowded Paris bus suddenly accuses his neighbour of deliberately bumping into him every time the bus stops to let people off, then flings himself into a seat that has become vacant; two hours later the narrator sees the same young man outside the Gare Saint-Lazare talking to an acquaintance who is apparently advising him to add an extra button on his overcoat. In reporting the story here, of course, I have actually also constructed a discourse, whose interpretive thrust emerges clearly in loaded expressions like 'accuses,' 'flings,' 'advising,' and so on. Queneau goes ninety-eight better: one story, ninety-nine 'different' discourses. But the quotation marks are necessary, for in one sense there is clearly only *one* discourse going on here rather than the ninety-nine with which we are so extravagantly presented. The real interest for the reader here, after all, is certainly not in the far less than fascinating *tranche de vie* so exhaustively described, but rather in how (and how long) Queneau – or his narrator (or is it ninety-nine narrators?) – will manage to keep up the highly self-reflexive game, keep the various discursive balls in the air without dropping them. There is what one might call a 'macrodiscourse,' in other words, which contains (or presents itself in the form of) ninety-nine separate 'microdiscourses.' The story of any one of the microdiscourses is the unchanging story of the irascible but fashion-conscious young commuter; the story of the text as a whole, however, is the story of the narrator's bravura performance. The discourse, in other words, *is* the story. For while ostensibly presenting the story no less than ninety-nine times – and who could reasonably ask for more than that? – the discourse (shades of Zeno) has in fact managed to push the story out of the way altogether, has triumphantly succeeded in usurping its place entirely in the reader's attention.

3

Discourse Discoursed:
The Ventriloquism Effect

The question as to whose voice we 'hear' telling us the story when we read a novel might initially seem to be so easy to answer as to preclude any further discussion. Simple questions, however, cannot always be simply answered, and it can now be admitted that our discussion in the last chapter of characters and their doings in time and space is very seriously deficient in one major aspect, since it provisionally operates on the implicit assumption that everything presented in the narrative text can be taken entirely at face value as the presentation of an ideally objective, unbiased, and ultimately *undivided* narrative voice. It is now time to abandon that entirely untenable assumption. No narrative voice, however apparently objective or unbiased, is *ever* undivided, for all narrative discourse, implicitly or explicitly, is *compound* discourse. The next three chapters will look at various aspects of this assertion. Let us begin in the present chapter by examining what we may call the *ventriloquism effect* in narrative, namely the inherently constitutive characteristic of all narrative discourse – though certainly actualized to a greater or a lesser degree in different kinds of narrative – that it essentially operates by disguising the point of origin of its discursive voice. To this end, we shall turn first to a consideration of the nature of narrators and narratees, then to the question of so-called implied authors and readers, and finally to the concept of compound discourse in general and its implications for the nature of narrative discourse.

NARRATORS

The most obvious example of the ventriloquism effect in narrative is the representation in a narrative text, by its narrator, of what is said (or thought) by its characters – where the primary voice of the narrator, that is to say, presents another, secondary voice, that of a character, speaking 'through' it. In order to do this, there are three basic possibilities at the disposal of any narrator: at one end of the scale, the narrator simply reports the utterance of a character as one more narrative event like any other ('John told Susan he loved her and always would'); at the other end of the scale, the narrator reports exactly what the character 'actually' said ('"I love you, Susan," John whispered. "I love you and I swear I always will'"); and, more interestingly, the narrator can also focus our attention on some intermediate point on that scale by apparently combining his or her own voice and that of the character ('John made his declaration to Susan that same evening. He loved her. He would always love her. Would she never understand that? Susan stared silently out the window'). In the first of these examples, the maximally *diegetic* option, we hear only the voice of the narrator, telling rather than showing, with John's voice not at all in evidence, just as if the narrator had said, 'John helped himself liberally and began to eat.' In the second, the maximally *mimetic* option, on the contrary, where the narrator elects to show what happened rather than tell about it, we hear, with the exception of the narrator's (optional) tag phrase simply identifying the speaker, only John's voice, as if we were physically present ourselves at the lovers' meeting. In the third option, finally, we have an example of an overtly mixed or compound discourse, where we again 'hear' what John said, but this time only at one remove, filtered, as it were, through the narrator's perception and presentation of it. In each of the first two examples there is only one voice present; in the third, exemplifying what Mieke Bal calls 'text interference' (1985: 142), we seem to hear two simultaneously, and an unambiguous attribution to the narrator on the one hand or the character on the other of what was 'really' said is frequently impossible. This form of speech representation – generally known as free indirect discourse – has generated much interest among narrative theorists for its ability to allow a third-person narrative to exploit a first-person point of view, and much more could be said about it.[1] For the moment, however, we may postpone any further discussion of the technical details until the chapter on focalization, since the latter plays a central role in discussing this particular textual phenomenon. What is of more immediate interest to us at this point is merely to note first of all the importance of compound discourse as a particular technical *device* at the disposal of a narrator. The concept of compound discourse, however, as we shall see, goes far beyond this limited (if still highly interesting) initial application.

All narratives are uttered, whether metaphorically or literally, by the voice of a narrator.[2] That voice may be presented as completely disembodied, that of a narrator who/which is nothing more than a voice, an *it* rather than a *he* or a *she*, entirely uninvolved in the events recounted; alternatively, it may be presented as that of a complexly developed character deeply involved in those events; or, yet again, it may occupy any one of a potentially infinite number of intermediate positions between these extremes involving perceived degrees of personality or abstraction, participation or non-participation, knowledge or ignorance, reliability or unreliability, independence or relativization. The standard classification of narrators currently in widest use is that of Gérard Genette (1980: 228–52), who employs two intersecting criteria: that of the narrative level on which the narrator operates and that of the narrator's participation or lack of it in the narrative reality presented. In terms of narrative level, since every narrator either produces or is part of a particular narrative reality — or, as Genette calls it, a *diegesis* – every narrative first of all has an *extradiegetic* narrator who produces it; any character within that primary narrative who also produces a narrative is an *intradiegetic* narrator; and any character within that (second-degree) narrative who produces a further (and thus third-degree) narrative is a *hypodiegetic* narrator.[3] Thus in Emily Brontë's *Wuthering Heights*, for example, Mr Lockwood is an extradiegetic narrator whose narrative includes Nelly Dean's intradiegetic narrative, which itself includes Isabella's hypodiegetic narrative. In terms of participation in the narrative reality presented, any one of these three kinds of narrator may either play a greater or lesser role as a character in his or her own narrative, in which case Genette speaks of a *homodiegetic* narrator, or may be entirely absent from it, in which case the narrator is said to be *heterodiegetic*. Genette's two criteria intersect: thus Lockwood is both extradiegetic and homodiegetic, since he plays a role, even if a relatively minor one, in his own narrative; Scheherazade is an intradiegetic narrator within the primary narrative of *The Arabian Nights* and also heterodiegetic, in that she plays no part in (most of) the stories she tells the king.

Genette's classification of narrators already makes abundantly clear the degree to which narrators can differ among themselves – and suggests also the degree to which the authority of at least some of these narratives may be rendered suspect by their relative position in the hierarchy of narrative levels and the degree of personal involvement on the part of their narrator. Whichever of the positions they may occupy on Genette's classificational grid, moreover, narrators also have further options as to how they may operate. A narrator may present himself more overtly, for example, by drawing the reader's attention to his own role and establishing very clearly what his own attitude and opinions are (as does the narrator, say, of Balzac's *Père Goriot*); or he may behave more covertly, by remaining in the background instead and keeping his opinions to himself (as does, say, the typical Hemingway narrator). And, most important of all, he or she may be or seem to be entirely reliable or alternatively entirely unreliable – or be situated at any point (or a succession of such points) on the scale between these two positions.[4]

As readers, we measure a narrator's objectivity and reliability primarily by our perception of the degree of his or her involvement in the narrative reality presented. In this context we may further distinguish, cutting across Genette's grid, two fundamentally different types of narrator, *character-narrators*, who figure as characters within a narrative, whether their own or another, and *external narrators*, who do not.[5] A character-narrator who appears as a character in his or her own narrative is, of course, both external to that narrative as its narrator, and, more important in this context, internal to it as a character – and therefore compromised as a narrator. Only narrators designated as both extradiegetic *and* heterodiegetic in Genette's classification are external narrators in this sense, and even then only to the extent that they acquire through their own discourse no more than a minimal degree of characterization; otherwise, like all other narrators (including extrahomodiegetic) they enter the ranks of character-narrators. The extradiegetic narrator of *Père Goriot* is an external narrator in this sense; Mr Lockwood in *Wuthering Heights*, however, though also extradiegetic, is a character-narrator.

An external narrator, always completely absent from the narrative reality he or she evokes, is instinctively credited by the reader with complete narrative authority and therefore complete objectivity. An external narrator such as we encounter in *Père Goriot* is both omniscient and omnipotent with regard to the narrative world inhabited by his characters; his narrative vision is both panchronic and ubiquitous, he can see into the future as easily as into the past or present, he can be present everywhere simultaneously, and he can see into the minds and hearts of his characters far better than they themselves ever can; moreover, he will never forget, never be confused or in error, never lie, and never twist his narrative to suit his own ends.[6] The character-narrator, on the other hand – Mr Lockwood, for example – is actually or potentially lacking on all of these scores, and his narrative is thus in principle *always* questionable, whereas that of the (truly) external narrator *never* is.

Our perception as readers as to whether we are dealing with an external narrator or a character-narrator is always crucial to our reading of the narrative he or she presents, whether we are consciously aware of this or not. In a sentence like 'Someone must have traduced Joseph K., for without having done anything wrong he was arrested one fine morning,' the opening sentence of Kafka's *Trial*, there are three possibilities that offer themselves to the reader as far as determining the reliability and objectivity of the narrator is concerned. First, the narrative voice may belong to an external narrator, whose account we shall tend to read as entirely objective unless we are given good reason to do otherwise. Second, the narrative voice may instead be that of a character-narrator who recounts from personal knowledge or hearsay the doings of his fellow character Joseph K., and whose narrative objectivity will certainly be coloured to some extent both by his limited knowledge and by his personal attitude towards K. Third, the narrative voice may belong to K. himself, referring to himself for whatever reason in the third person rather than the first, and thus tend to be read as the least objective, most subjective of the three voices. The systemic indeterminacy that characterizes Kafka's narrative style, indeed, is very largely due precisely to his reader's inability to decide definitively on just one of these interpretive options.

So far, however, we have been tacitly assuming that there is a narrative gold standard against which the reliability or otherwise of a narrator may be measured. Balzac's narrator in *Père Goriot*, sovereignly detached and distanced from the action he describes, inspires complete confidence in his narrative reliability and is very unlikely to forfeit that confidence. A character-narrator like David Balfour in Robert Louis Stevenson's *Kidnapped*, caught up himself in the events he speaks of, will retain the reader's confidence only as long as he does not seem to be colouring his narrative more than the narrated circumstances would appear to warrant. He may indeed turn out to be entirely unreliable, but his lack of reliability will emerge by contrast with what the reader is led by the text as a whole to assume would be a more reasonable course of events.

Very different from the always possible local unreliability of any character-narrator is the flaunted systemic unreliability we encounter with a narrator who is unreliable not because he wishes to conceal some truth or propagate some falsehood relevant to the story he is telling but because his narrative calls in question the whole concept of narrative reliability. We encounter such a self-questioning, self-undermining narrator in Samuel Beckett's

Molloy (1951), whose very dubious reliability as a narrator is established by such comments as the following: 'A little dog followed him, a pomeranian I think, but I don't think so. I wasn't sure at the time and I'm still not sure, though I've hardly thought about it' (11); 'I must have been on the top, or on the slopes, of some considerable eminence, for otherwise how could I have seen, so far away, so near at hand, so far beneath, so many things, fixed and moving. But what was an eminence doing in this land with hardly a ripple? And I, what was I doing there, and why come?' (14); 'And every time I say, I said this, or I said that ... and then a fine phrase more or less clear and simple ... I am merely complying with the convention that demands you either lie or hold your peace. For what really happened was quite different' (88).

Another kind of systemic narrative unreliability, not always recognized as such, emerges in the case of multiple narrators. Many narratives have several narrators, whether following one another sequentially or, much more interestingly, with one narrator's account embedded within that of another. William Faulkner's *The Sound and the Fury* (1929) provides an example of sequential narrators, where the reader's understanding of the narrative grows only gradually out of his efforts to compare and contrast a series of partially conflicting accounts by three separate narrators – who are moreover all to a greater or lesser degree unreliable, consisting as they do of an imbecile, a potential suicide, and a bad-tempered bigot. Conrad's *Heart of Darkness* and Emily Brontë's *Wuthering Heights*, for their part, provide interesting examples of embedded narratives. Usually the relationship between such nested narratives is ostensibly quite clear, with the embedded narrative playing a clearly subsidiary role, simply providing one more item of narrative material for the larger narrative in which it is embedded. Thus in many pre-realist texts (like, say, *Don Quixote*) many of the embedded narratives could be deleted without any significant damage to the structural integrity of the embedding narrative. In *Heart of Darkness*, however, we find a reversal of this power relationship, where the character Marlow's account of his adventures in Africa, though presented in the form of an intradiegetic narrative, is clearly much more important than the extradiegetic narrative in which it is contained and which essentially serves only as a frame for it.

Such narrative embeddedness is interesting in our present context in that it highlights the vital question as to whose voice we are *really* (which, of course, is to say metaphorically) 'hearing' as we read the narrative account. *Wuthering Heights* provides a particularly interesting example of multiple embedded narratives, Mr Lockwood's extradiegetic narrative embedding a lengthy oral narrative in several instalments by the servant Nelly Dean as well as a written narrative by Catherine Earnshaw (32–4), and Nelly's intradiegetic narrative in turn further embedding three separate narratives, by Isabella (151–60), Heathcliff (241–3), and the servant Zillah (244–5) respectively. Thus Isabella's hypodiegetic oral narrative, for example, though it appears on the page in quotation marks as if issuing directly from her lips, 'actually' reaches the reader only at two removes, filtered first through Nelly Dean's likewise oral account to Mr Lockwood and then through the written narrative of Mr Lockwood himself. So who is really 'narrating' here? Is it more important that we are reading what Isabella said, or what Nelly says she said, or what Mr Lockwood says Nelly said she said? How many possible alterations of style, emphasis, effect, and perhaps even fact may in principle have taken place in this multiple transmission? Whichever way we may wish to decide such questions as readers, however, it is clear that the relationship between nested narratives is always one of mutual relativization: while the embedding narrative is ultimately always in a position to colour fundamentally our reception of an embedded narrative, it may itself always in turn be challenged or even displaced altogether by the narrative it embeds. This mutual relativization, moreover, as we shall see, is by no means limited to cases involving an actual hypodiegetic narrative but rather is entirely typical of narrative as a discursive system, for in an important sense narratological theory requires us to read *every* narrative in terms of its embeddedness. The situation of embeddedness, indeed, as I shall argue over the next three chapters, far from being just some incidental structural luxury to be employed occasionally for special effect, is the central structural characteristic of all narrative.

IMPLIED AUTHORS

The narrator as such, however reliable he/she/it may in fact prove to be, cannot be said to be the ultimately authoritative source of the narrative we encounter as readers. This is especially obvious in the case of a narrative like, say, *The Sound and the Fury*, with its multiple unreliable narratives. Since we can rely on no one of the three narratives but can none the less – as much in spite of as because of the individual narrators' accounts – form an opinion as to what 'must' be the real story behind the distorting accounts of it, it follows that there must be some agency 'behind' the narrative voice that directs us towards that synthesis. Narrative theorists have designated that agency the *implied author*, a narrative agent to be seen as identical neither with any narrator nor with the real author.[7] The implied author emerges only from our overall reading of the positions, values, and opinions espoused by the narrative text as a whole, reconstructed by that reading as the semiotically necessary authorial *stance* demanded by this particular text. These opinions and values may or may not be the same as those of the real author, for clearly an author who rejected capital punishment, for example, could none the less write a work that fully espoused it. For this reason it is also evident that *every* book of, say, Kafka has its own particular implied author, whose opinions may differ sharply in each case from those of the real author: our picture of the author Kafka, indeed (as opposed to the *man* Kafka), is made up precisely of our composite picture of all the individual implied authors of all the Kafka texts we have read, modified by the critical opinions of other readers (friends, teachers, critics) whose Kafka is also constructed by just the same process. The implied author is also clearly not identical with the extradiegetic narrator, since we judge the narrator's reliability or otherwise by recourse to our image of what the implied author evidently really intends us to understand: the trustworthiness of any extradiegetic narrator varies as the perceived distance between the narrator and the implied author. Without an implied author to provide such a narrative gold standard, indeed, we would have no way to gauge a narrator's unreliability in the first place (Chatman 1978: 149).

But, since every text, including every narrative, obviously has a *real* author, is it actually necessary to postulate such an agent as the *implied* author in the first place? Indeed, not all narrative theorists *do* subscribe to the notion that an implied author is a necessary agent in the narrative situation. Both Bal (1985: 119–20) and Rimmon-Kenan (1983: 88), for example, specifically exclude the concept of the implied author as a valid concern of narratology: for the notion of the implied author, as Bal writes, is 'not limited to narrative texts, but is of application to any text' and is consequently 'not specific to narratology, which has ... as its objective the narrative aspects of a narrative text' (120). While so strict a definition of the scope of narrative theory certainly has its uses, however, it has its obvious limitations also, and while it is perfectly reasonable to ask if implied authors, like Santa Claus, can really be said to exist at all, the more pertinent question is really not so much whether there *is* such a narrative entity as whether it is useful to *postulate* its existence, to act *as if* such an entity existed.

Clearly, the crucial usefulness of the implied author is that he or she – or, even better, *it*, since we are speaking here essentially of an inferred authorial *stance* – provides us with a notional norm of *authority* within the text itself, against which narratorial deviations can be gauged. Lacking the implied author, we necessarily have to look for that authority either outside the text in the authorial intention of the real author or inside the text in the person of the narrator. The first of these options, though a staple of traditional pre-formalist criticism, has been entirely justifiably discredited as an all too blunt critical instrument; the second option, though superficially preferable in that it locates authority inside rather than outside the text, is equally lacking in the ability to make fine distinctions; both options are fundamentally flawed in that they place altogether too much emphasis on the idea of a real and undivided *person*, outside or inside the text respectively, who *means* exactly what he or she *says*. As we have already seen, however, the concept of an undivided, univocal narrative voice is a drastic oversimplification.

As so often, a major part of the problem is in the terms we use: we generally think of 'narration,' reasonably enough, as an action performed by a 'narrator.' In fact, however, *narration* in the strict sense – and which we may define as the process of transforming *story* into *text* – might more usefully be thought of as the combination of a number of acts of *arrangement* performed by the *implied author*, involving the following essential elements: (a) *chronologization*, or the arrangement of time, transforming action into plot; (b) *localization*, or the arrangement of space, transforming place into setting; (c) *characterization*, or the arrangement of personality traits, transforming actors into characters; (d) *focalization*, or the arrangement of narrative perspective; (e) *verbalization*, or the arrangement of words on the page, making *all* of the implied author's arrangements known to the reader – and duly received by the reader as the 'voice' of the narrator; and (f) *validation* of the narrator's degree of reliability. Even in the case of the most obviously objective external narrator, that is to say, what we normally think of as an entirely univocal narrator is thus always more accurately thought of as being a *compound* narrative instance, composed of the implied author as the 'director' behind the narrative and the narrator as its 'performer.' In this view, therefore, everything on the level of text – the organization of events, time, space, and character development – is indeed produced by the voice of the narrator, but everything the narrator does is made possible in the first place only by the prior activity of the implied author. The extradiegetic narrator's essential, indeed *only* role is to make the implied author's inventions perceptible, for if there were no narrator the implied author would be forever beyond reach, condemned to total inability to communicate.

The relationship between the implied author and the narrator is thus an essentially ironic one – demonstrating once again the implicitly ludic element in narrative structure – for while the narrator always deals in semantic information, the implied author, as 'silent narrator' behind the narrative voice, always deals in the signal information that tells us how the semantic information should be understood (Lyons 1977: 41). As one might say, the implied author is thus a *gnomon*, what is left of narration after the narrating *voice* is taken away, otherwise definable as the difference between what the text *says* and what we take it as *meaning*.[8]

Pre-formalist readers routinely subsumed this double narrative agency under the common-sense label of the 'author' and unproblematically equated it with the real flesh-and-blood author, just as even theoretically sophisticated readers will occasionally say things like 'As Tolstoy says in *Anna Karenina*, "All happy families resemble one another, but each unhappy family is unhappy in its own way."' And in an appropriate context, of course, this is a perfectly reasonable thing to say, even though Tolstoy wrote not in English but in Russian and even though several generations of more sophisticated readers, in the wake of Anglo-American New Criticism, conscientiously learned to attribute such opinions to the 'narrator' instead, denying in effect that Tolstoy could say anything at all in *Anna Karenina*. The argument outlined here would suggest that, at least in this respect, the apparently more sophisticated formalist view is in fact little more so than its predecessor.

It might, of course, be objected that the whole notion of an 'implied' author is merely terminological hair-splitting, an unnecessary and self-indulgent exercise in counting the number of narrative agents that can dance on the point of a narratological pin. Such an argument, however, ignores the complexity of narrative both as a literary genre and as a semiotic system. The reason why the implied author is a relatively new arrival on the narratological scene is reasonably obvious: for traditional realist readers, essentially convinced of the authority, veracity, and sincerity of the 'real' author, the signal information and the semantic information of the authorial 'message' were always perceived to be essentially consonant. As irony, parody, and assorted other forms of duplicity began to be the narratorial norm for modernist and post-modernist writing (and reading), the 'invention' of the implied author as a regulatory mechanism became inevitable.

The concept of the implied author has to do most importantly with narrative authority and its location. For the pre-formalist reader, the 'I' who acted in a story and the 'I' who related the story were essentially the same, and common sense made it obvious that 'I' was the empirical or real author. The introduction of the narrator by critics of a formalist turn of mind disrupted that identity and dislocated the focus of narrative authority from the author to the now more distanced narrator. The further introduction of the implied author essentially dispossesses the narrator of authority in the same way as the narrator had formerly dispossessed the author. One might be tempted to see this in traditionalist terms as evidence merely of the focus of narrative authority reverting to where it really belonged, namely with the real author. As the real author dissolves in a web of post-formalist intertextuality, however, the shift allows itself to be seen more clearly in its true colours, namely as a potentially infinite regress (which is to say, dispersal) of authority.

For while it is methodologically convenient to regard the implied author as the ultimate intratextual guarantor of the narrator's reliability, it is evident that we must also, in the end, admit the possibility of an *unreliable implied author*. The implied author of Robbe-Grillet's *La Maison de Rendez-vous* would be an example of this, in that the structure of the narration in that text undermines the very notion of authority. (One could indeed say that it is precisely the unreliability of the implied author that has come to typify post-modernist narrative.) Such an entity is in effect an *implied implied author,* since his or her unreliability can in turn be assessed only by recourse to the reliability of a 'real' implied author. But this latter could also be unreliable – and so on. Ultimately, of course, this is merely a restatement of the evident fact that all narration is always unreliable to at least some degree, in that any narration is the result of the adoption, in a particular narrative context, of a particular narrative position and perspective, for particular narrative ends. Any certainty we might hope to reach with regard to narration, in other words, emerges as nothing more than a summation of a potentially endless series of narrative uncertainties.

SENDERS AND RECEIVERS

Once again, however, in our presentation of the narrator and the implied author, we have been guilty of deliberately suppressing some of the relevant narratological evidence. For neither the narrator nor the implied author is the only agent involved in the narrative transaction on the relevant diegetic level. Narrative, after all, is a communication, and as such it presupposes not only a sender (such as the narrator and/or the implied author) and a message (namely the narrative text we read) but also, in each case, a receiver. Storytelling, after all, is a two-way affair. Not only is the story 'told' on the respective diegetic levels by the narrator, the implied author, and, lest we forget, also by a real live author; there is, as we have already seen in an earlier chapter, another kind of 'telling' going on too. It is evident that from the linguistic signs and cultural clues afforded by the author's text the *reader*, for a start, is able to 'tell' what is going on – and narrative theorists extend this analogy to the relationship between both the narrator and his or her 'reader,' namely the *narratee*, and the implied author and his or her 'reader,' namely the *implied reader*. We therefore end up with a discursive trinity of sender-tellers as well as a corresponding triad of receiver-tellers — not to mention the obvious fact that characters can also tell each other stories, even embedded (and even multiply embedded) stories as well. We shall now go on to examine some of the implications of this multiple, stereophonic, polyvocal telling, this multiple interplay of sender-tellers and receiver-tellers, projectors and receivers. Let us begin with the narrator-narratee pair, move then to the implied author and implied reader, and finally take only a very preliminary look at the relationship between the real author and the real reader, a relationship to which we shall, however, return in more detail in a later chapter. (Not all narratologists would necessarily agree with this procedure, as already noted, for though most would begin with the same first pair, some would

disqualify the second pair as unnecessary, and most would exclude the third pair as already beyond the appropriate concerns
of narratology in the strict sense.)[9]

Narrators do not narrate into a void. Their narratives, most contemporary narratologists agree, are addressed to an audience, a
narratee, on the same diegetic level. Extradiegetic narrators thus
narrate for extradiegetic narratees, intradiegetic narrators for
intradiegetic narratees. Likewise, character-narrators narrate for
character-narratees, and external narrators for external narratees.
The same character, evidently, can function both as narrator and
as narratee: thus, in *Wuthering Heights*, Nelly functions as both
narrator to Lockwood and narratee to Isabella, Heathcliff, and
Zillah; while Lockwood is both narratee to Nelly Dean and narrator to that eventual reader presupposed by his written narrative. This eventual reader, narratee to Lockwood's narrator, we
should be quite clear, is *not* the real reader, namely you or I, for
Lockwood is a character in a fiction, and his narratee, located by
definition on the same diegetic level, can only be another character – though, as in many narratives, the narratee in *Wuthering
Heights* is in fact left unrealized as a character. If Lockwood left
his journal lying about, for example, it could well be found and
read by Nelly Dean or any one of the other characters, just as
Lockwood himself finds and reads Catherine Earnshaw's narrative. The real reader is called upon to play a similar role to that of
the narratee, but that is the extent of the similarity, for the real
reader knows that Heathcliff and Lockwood are fictions, while
the narratee (say, Nelly Dean finding the manuscript) knows that
they are real people. Alternatively, of course, Lockwood might
never have intended his account to be read by anyone else in the
first place – but in this case Lockwood himself is narratee as well
as narrator.

Though literary critics have long since distinguished narrators
from authors, the necessary existence of narratees as an element
in the narrative situation was first clearly stated only in 1971 by
Gerald Prince, and subsequently elaborated by Genette (1972:
265; 1980: 259). Since the narratee's role is purely receptive, it
might well seem that his or her role is entirely passive and there-

fore negligible. Such is not the case, however, for, as Genette observes (1980: 260), a narrative is always addressed to someone, even if only the narrator him- or herself, and therefore always has a particular thrust or appeal, aims at a particular effect, desires a particular response. This shaping of the narrative by the narrator's expectation of the narratee's response can be seen in such situations as the scene in Theodor Fontane's *Effi Briest* (1895), where Effi, recently separated from her husband, is told by her doctor to send her old servant Roswitha for him whenever he is needed. '"Just send Roswitha," Rummschüttel had said. And does that mean that Roswitha was in Effi's employ, then? ... She was indeed' (310; trans. mine). The voice that asks the question here is certainly that of the narrator, since the narrator's voice is the only voice we ever hear, but the question is evidently one the narrator assumes his narratee would wish to have answered. The result is a further ventriloquism effect: the narrator speaks with what he assumes is the voice of his narratee – a fully involved narratee, we notice, who thus, as far as Fontane is concerned, stands in for a possibly less deeply involved reader, one who might otherwise have missed the relatively small point that Roswitha, who had been separated from Effi for several months, had by now returned to her service.

The implied author, to transfer this receptive analogy to the next higher diegetic level, might in fact just as accurately be described as the 'inferred' author, for since 'he' is completely without any voice other than that of the narrator, his profile emerges only gradually from our *reading* of the narrative, implied by the positions and values the text is inferred to espouse.[10] The implied author, in other words, is *created* by our reading, as real readers, of the narrative text, created, in fact, as the very *possibility of any particular reading*. To read a particular text as ironic, for example, is to *imply* an author whose text allows such a reading as well as to *infer* the possible existence of that author *from* our reading. It will therefore be evident that ultimately every text has as many implied authors as it has real readers. It will also be evident, however, that I cannot simply decide entirely arbitrarily to read *Oedipus Rex* or *King Lear* as a farce. To be more accurate, I can of

course decide to do so, but my resulting reading will be hope-
lessly inadequate, utterly idiosyncratic, and entirely deficient in
any ability to persuade other readers of its validity. One of the
most important reasons for my critical failure in this scenario
will be my decision to ignore yet another entity in the narrative
transaction, namely the implied reader, who stands in the same
relationship to the implied author as does the narratee to the
narrator.

Every literary text, as read by particular individual readers,
demands a particular reading – or, in other words, implies a
particular reader. This implied reader, like the implied author, is
again identified by the real reader, since real readers will, of
course, see the 'same' text as demanding quite different readings
– if this were not the case, after all, the entire academic industry
of literary criticism would be impossible. There will none the less
be a reasonable degree of similarity between these divergent
readings to the extent that readers belong, in Stanley Fish's phrase,
to the same interpretive community (1980: 14), though different
interpretive communities may, and do, differ significantly among
themselves. (My reading of *King Lear* as farce would fail essentially because of its too great distance from the readings of all
currently existing interpretive communities. Such a failed reading identifies an implied reader who does not yet exist; his or her
eventual existence, however – as the result of a continuing series
of less radically 'foreign' readings – should not necessarily be
excluded.)

Mirroring the relationship of the real author and the implied
author, the relationship of the real reader and the implied reader
is that of a real person and a reconstructed necessary receptive
stance: the implied reader is the reader 'called for' by the text,
just as the implied author is the author 'called for' in its production. Likewise, the implied reader, too, is a gnomon, for as the
(reliable) narrator 'says' what the implied author 'means,' so the
narratee 'hears' what the implied reader 'sees' the implied author as meaning: the implied reader, in other words, is the difference between content and signal, between 'hears' and 'sees.' Like
the implied author, too, the implied reader, as already suggested,

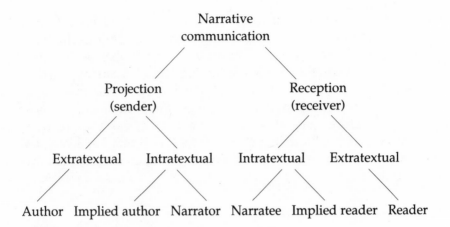

Figure 3.1 Narrative senders, narrative receivers

is constructed by the real reader – or rather, in a paradoxical hermeneutic interactivity, *re*constructed via our understanding of the implied reader constructed by the real author, whom in turn we reach only through the implied author, constructed by us.

As our discussion of the roles of the narratee and the implied reader might suggest, narrative communication – like literary communication in general – operates essentially according to the *principle of interactivity*, where the narrative 'message' is constituted not just by its sender(s) but also and simultaneously by its receiver(s). Only the intratextual senders and receivers have generally been considered legitimate matters of concern for the classical narratologist, concerned exclusively with the structural workings of the text in a narrower sense. Post-structural narrative theory, however, widens its focus to allow consideration of questions involving, for example, the role of authorial and readerly intention as constitutive factors in the textual transaction – and again this is an area to which we shall return in a later chapter. The overall interrelationship of senders and receivers, however, can meanwhile be portrayed as in figure 3.1.

Narrative structure, of course, is in one sense merely a convenient fiction — but then so are the theorems of philosophy, psychology, and mathematics. The point to remember is that they are *useful*, productive fictions, allowing us to investigate various classes of phenomena, including textual phenomena, in particular lights, from particular perspectives, for particular purposes. Let us therefore conclude our consideration of narration as compound discourse by telling another story, one that looks at some of the relationships we have discussed so far in a somewhat different light.

NARRATIVE AS VENTRILOQUISM

According to Wolfgang Kayser, once we lose sight of the notion that the narrator is 'someone' who 'tells a story,' the novel is dead: 'The death of the narrator is the death of the novel' (1954: 34; my translation). So far in our discussion, for the sake of convenience, the narrator and the other entities in the narrative transaction have been treated more or less in anthropomorphic terms, more or less as if they were real persons. It is possible to see their mode of being and their relationships quite differently, however – and in a way that once again underlines what we have been calling the ventriloquism effect in narration.

An *actant*, in A.-J. Greimas's semiotic terminology, is a vacant conceptual slot in a narrative structure waiting to be filled, an abstract narrative function – similar to such standard grammatical concepts as 'subject' or 'object' – waiting to be concretely realized by one or more *actors*.[11] Greimas's concept of such actantial roles is most usually discussed in the context of story-grammar, but it has been usefully extended to the discursive levels of text and narration as well (cf. Prince 1989: 2). The notion of such *discourse actants* allows us to look at the relationship of intradiegetic and extradiegetic narrators, for example, in something of a new light. The actantial role of, say, the 'subject' (the protagonist of a narrative) in Greimas's model of story-grammar is actually concretized on two different narrative levels: as actor on the level of story, and as character on the level of text. The process of narration likewise becomes apparent on two levels, though in some cases this is considerably more obvious than in others. In any narrative, the most obviously indispensable narrative role is that of narrator, for a story can become a story only by being told. When we talk of the *narrator* here, however, we might remember that we are really talking about the concretization of a necessary *narrative actant* (which, if we wished to coin a term, we might call a *narratant*, where the pair *narratant/narrator* would correspond to Greimas's *actant/actor*). For in some narratives the narrating voice is internal (intradiegetic), projected, that is to say, as the voice of a character within the story told, while in others the narrating voice is external, belonging to a world outside of that occupied by the characters of the narrative text. Where the narrative voice is made to come from, however, is in one sense a trick of ventriloquism, the result of the fact that, just as story-level actants are concretized on two different levels (story and text), what we might call the narratant is also always potentially concretized on both the level of text and that of narration.

Thus, the narrative transaction – the overall interactive process of production of a narrative text – might be visualized in terms of a narrative scale that would include all seven transactional points operative in the narrative transaction, namely author, implied author, narrator, character, narratee, implied reader, and reader. This scale is bidirectional, the process of narrative projection directed from the position of author to that of reader, while that of reception is directed from the position of reader to that of author. In these terms, the narrator is thus neither a person nor even a character but rather a *narrative position*, a position or point on the narrative scale, situated between the level of the implied author and that of character, potentially coincident with either or neither of these, and seen as identifying the point of utterance of the narrative voice. The narratee, likewise, is the point of reception of the narrative voice, that transactional point on the narrative scale at which the narrative voice is seen to be aimed; situated again between the level of character and that of the implied reader and again potentially coincident with either or neither of these. The implied author is that transactional point seen as the locus of

A	A'	N	C	N'	R'	R

<---- EN/CN ---->| <----CN'/EN' --->

Figure 3.2 Narrative shifters

authority in a given text, and the implied reader that point seen as the locus of reception of a given text – where the word *seen* is deliberately ambiguous with regard to the question 'seen by whom?' since both the real author (the empirical sender) and the real reader (the empirical receiver) are interactively involved in their (re)construction.

Both the narrator and the narratee in this scenario are thus seen as unstable, non-fixed, shifters, as suggested in figure 3.2. The narrative voice belongs 'naturally' at position N (narrator), but can be 'thrown' so that it appears to come either from position C (character) or position A' (implied author), is repositioned *as if* it belonged to one or the other, in which case we call it a character-narrator (CN) or an external narrator (EN) respectively. The perceived 'proper' point of reception varies accordingly, with position N' (narratee) likewise potentially variable between coincidence with position C (character) and position R' (implied reader), in which case we speak respectively of a character-narratee (CN') or an external narratee (EN'). Occasionally, as when we recognize an unreliable narrator, we are allowed as readers to sense this hesitation between alternative possibilities, to glimpse the compound agency involved in the ostensibly univocal narrative voice.

Seeing narrators and narratees as operating simultaneously on *both* the extradiegetic and the intradiegetic level, indeed, can at least occasionally provide us with a useful tool. Second-person narration, for example, can cause a significant imbalance in the reader's perception of how the narrative text works, as excited reviewers of Italo Calvino's *If on a Winter's Night a Traveler* discovered as early as its opening sentence: 'You are about to begin reading Italo Calvino's new novel, *If on a winter's night a traveler*

... Best to close the door; the TV is always on in the next room' (3). If this sentence began with 'he was' or 'he is' instead of 'you are,' the matter would be entirely unproblematic, namely, to adopt a simple notation,

$$EN/CN\ (C_{he})\ EN'/CN'.$$

With 'you' instead of 'he,' it is entirely possible to construe the situation in exactly the same way:

$$EN/CN\ (C_{you})\ EN'/CN'$$

(cf. Prince 1982: 20), but, judging by Calvino's reviewers, few readers do. A more complex reading of the situation seems to be demanded by the pronoun 'you,' since 'you,' unlike 'he,' always carries the implication of a narratee. If we choose (and it *is* a matter of choice) to read 'you' as a character-narratee rather than merely as a character, and to read every narrative act as theoretically involving all *four* of EN, CN, CN', and EN', it becomes clear that our sense of imbalance as readers has to do on the one hand with perceived degrees of overtness and covertness among these narrative agents and, on the other, with the perceived possibility of what Genette would call a metalepsis, a mixing of narrative levels. Since the narrative voice has not yet characterized itself in any overt way as anything other than an objectively reporting voice, our first reaction as readers is to classify it, until further notice, as that of a *covert external narrator*, since an external narrator is always perceived, as we have seen, to be have greater narrative authority than a character-narrator, whose actantial role thus remains unmarked, again until possible further notice. 'You,' however, is clearly situated on the level of story, as a quite tangible character disturbed by the noise of the TV, and it is thus evident that we are dealing with an *overt character-narratee*, while the actantial role of external narratee remains for the moment unmarked. The relationship of imbalance might thus be described as follows:

$$\{EN\ (covert) \rightarrow \text{CN (unmarked)}\} \rightarrow \{CN'(overt) \rightarrow EN'\text{(unmarked)}\}.$$

That the imbalance is perceived rather than 'real' is clear from the fact that we *can* simply read 'you' as a character; that the perception *is* the reality is made a little clearer by the use of models of narrative structure that are flexible and dynamic rather than static and prescriptive.

But we do not need such elaborate examples to make the point that we are continually presented in narrative with 'voices' that come (or seem to come) from quite unexpected locations. We may conclude with two simpler, but in their way quite fascinating examples. First, it is possible for a narrator to 'report' the discourse of a character without actually using a word of it, as we see in the following example from Flaubert:

'It is very likely,' answered Homais, raising his eyebrows and putting on his weightiest expression, 'that the Seine-Inférieure Agricultural Show will this year be held at Yonville-l'Abbaye ... However, we'll talk of it another time. No, I can see my way, thank you; Justin has the lamp.' (*Madame Bovary* 135)

Homais is talking to Charles Bovary here, and although we do not hear Bovary utter a syllable we immediately grasp what he *must* have said. Homais's last sentence is obviously in response to an offer from Bovary to show him the way as he leaves Bovary's door by night. The reader must mentally supply this entirely elliptically reported offer, however, whose very existence is deducible only from the response it ostensibly evokes – the same technique is commonly employed in later fiction in reporting one-sided telephone conversations.

An equally unobtrusive but utterly effective piece of ventriloquism involves, for example, the use of a definite rather than an indefinite article, as in the following extract from John Le Carré's *A Small Town in Germany* (1969):

The plump man paused, leaned forward as if to examine something in the window; glanced down the road; and in that moment the light from the window shone full upon his features. The smaller man ran forward: stopped; ran forward again; and was too late.

The limousine had drawn up, an Opel Rekord driven by a pale man hidden in the smoked glass. (7)

The force of *'the* limousine' here, rather than *'a* limousine,' is to show us rather than tell us about the limousine, which is mentioned here for the first time; to assist in shiftng our attention to the 'smaller man' pursuing the first one (a shift completed by the word 'hidden'); and, of course, typically for narratives where (as here) readerly disorientation is a narrative goal, it also puts the reader at a disadvantage, for if *'a* limousine' allows the reader (erroneously) to think that he and the narrator both become aware of the vehicle's appearance simultaneously, *'the* limousine' makes clear what is in fact always true, namely that in matters of factual detail the reader is always and inevitably at least one step behind the narrative voice. Le Carré achieves a similar effect half a dozen pages later by introducing a new character as 'Cork, the albino cypher clerk' (13), where again the definite article subtly suggests that the reader should somehow have *known* already that Cork was both a cypher clerk and an albino. Spy novels achieve their major effect by the controlled unsettling of the reader; it is illuminating that that effect can be established by such apparently insignificant means. Information is not being withheld here; on the contrary, it is being proffered; but the reader is made to *feel* as if the information *has been* withheld up to this point, thus suggesting the further possibility that much other information may also be withheld by a narrator whose role as manipulator, as narrative ventriloquist, is now, however implicitly, established.

It will thus be very evident from the discussion in this chapter that no matter how simple and straightforward a narrative may initially appear to be, it *can* never be a single, undivided discourse. We have still examined only the tip of the discursive iceberg, however. The rest of the iceberg includes the concept of *focalization*, to which we will turn in our next chapter. It also includes two further and interlinked concepts that powerfully extend the range of the issues so far discussed, and which we will take up in a later chapter. The first of these is the concept of *metatextuality*, the second that of *intertextuality*. The presence of a symmetrically arranged triad of senders and receivers on three different diegetic levels results in a semiotic *mise en abyme*, a Chinese-boxes model of narrative levels suggesting an essential metatextual embeddedness and self-relativization within all narrative texts, whatever extratextual referentiality they may also have. Post-structuralist theorists of narrative such as Barthes and Kristeva, moreover, have advanced that analogy to the extratextual level as well, seeing not just the intratextual narrative but also the very writing and reading of all narratives as further embedded in an intertextual discourse, an endless interweaving and interwovenness of discursive voices without number, past, present, and to come.

4

Points of Origin:
The Focalization Factor

The subversive potential of what we have been calling the ventriloquism effect, involving the inherent dividedness of the narrative voice, is closely paralleled by what we may now call the focalization factor, involving the inherent dividedness of the narrative *vision* we, as readers, associate with that voice. Focalization, indeed, as Mieke Bal writes, is 'the most important, most penetrating, and most subtle means of manipulation' available to the narrative text, whether literary or otherwise (1985: 116). Yet both the intensive study of focalization in the narrower sense and even the expression itself were very late arrivals on the narratological scene.[1] The term, like so many others, was introduced into critical discourse only twenty years ago by Gérard Genette, in order, as he says himself, to dispel 'a regrettable confusion' surrounding an 'apparently obvious but almost universally disregarded distinction,' namely that 'between the question *Who is the character whose point of view orients the narrative perspective?* and the very different question *Who is the narrator? –* or, more simply, the question *Who sees?* and the question *Who speaks?*' (1980: 186). There had, of course, been a very considerable amount of critical discussion of the effects of 'narrative perspective' and 'point of view' in narrative, especially in the English-speaking world, long before Genette, who duly acknowledges the major contributions of such predecessors as Percy Lubbock, Cleanth Brooks and Robert Penn Warren, F.K. Stanzel, and Wayne Booth. None of these earlier contributions, however, made consistent use of the crucial distinction that informs all subsequent discussion of what we can call focalization in the narrower sense, namely, once again in the words of Mieke Bal, who considerably developed Genette's original system, 'the insight that the agent that sees must be given a status other than that of the agent that narrates' (1985: 101).

Focalization is a matter of mediation. As Shlomith Rimmon-Kenan puts it with exemplary brevity, 'the story is presented in the text through the mediation of some "prism," "perspective," "angle of vision," verbalized by the narrator though not necessarily his' (1983: 71), and this mediation is what Genette and his followers call focalization.[2] The fundamental distinction between verbalization and focalization emerges very clearly, to repeat an often used example, in the opening sentence of Joyce's *Portrait of the Artist* (1916):

Once upon a time and a very good time it was there was a moocow coming down along the road and this moocow that was coming down along the road met a nicens little boy named baby tuckoo ... (7)

Here the narrative voice is, as always, that of the narrator, but the perceptions conveyed are those of the very young child Stephen listening to a bedtime story. Voice and vision, in other words, quite clearly derive from separate points of origin. By contrast, the opening sentence of Thackeray's *Vanity Fair* (1848) is clearly both narrated and focalized from the same centre of consciousness, voice and vision sharing a common point of origin:

While the present century was in its teens, and on one sunshiny morning in June, there drove up to the great iron gate of Miss Pinkerton's academy for young ladies, on Chiswick Mall, a large family coach, with two fat horses in blazing harness, driven by a fat coachman in a three-cornered hat and wig, at the rate of four miles an hour. (11)

Like *Vanity Fair*, Dostoevsky's *Crime and Punishment* (1866), to take a final example, also opens with a sentence where both the narrative voice and the focalization appear at first reading to be clearly those of the narrator and the narrator alone:

Towards the end of a sultry afternoon early in July a young man came out of his little room in Stolyarny Lane and turned slowly and somewhat irresolutely in the direction of Kamenny Bridge. (1)

Only the phrase 'and somewhat irresolutely' may give us some slight pause here – but that will be quite enough to introduce surprisingly radical doubts, whether acknowledged or not, into our reading of Dostoevsky's opening statement, doubts that the reader of Thackeray's opening sentence has no reason to entertain. Where is Raskolnikov's alleged irresolution being 'seen' from? Is it something that is known to the narrator because the narrator, as in *Vanity Fair*, is omniscient and can thus see, godlike, into the minds of all his characters? Or is it rather that Raskolnikov's lack of resolve was in fact clearly visible *physically* to the narrator, who just happened, as a fellow character, to be standing across the street on that July afternoon watching the young man leave his lodgings? Or is there, after all, an at least momentary divergence between the narrating voice and the perceiving eye, as in Joyce's *Portrait*, allowing us a sudden and unexpected glimpse through Raskolnikov's own eyes, if only for the duration of the three words in question? The attempt to answer such questions leads us directly to the central consideration of what focalization theory can and cannot do for us as readers of a narrative text. Before going any further, however, let us attempt to establish some of the ground rules by which the game of focalization is played.

ASPECTS OF FOCALIZATION

To begin with terminology, the story is presented – transformed into the narrative text – through a double mediation, namely a 'voice' that 'speaks' and 'eyes' that 'see': the former belonging to the narrator (whether actualized as a disembodied narrative voice or as a more or less personalized character-narrator), the latter to the *focalizer*, the perceived centre of consciousness, 'who' may or may not, as we have seen, be identical with the narrator. It is important to understand, however, that to speak in anthropomorphic terms of a 'focalizer,' with 'eyes,' is purely a convenient metaphorical strategy. The focalizer is not a 'person,' not even an agent in the same way that the narrator or implied author is a narrative agent, but rather a chosen *point*, the point from which the narrative is perceived as being presented at any given moment.[3]

This point of origin may be perceived as *external* or *internal* to the story presented. The focalizer of the opening sentence of *Vanity Fair*, for example, is clearly external to the events presented, while the focalizer of the opening sentence of *A Portrait of the Artist* is clearly internal, a participant in the events narrated by the narrator. We may refer to the former of these as external focalization (EF) and to the latter as internal focalization (IF). The external focalizer will, of course, usually be a narrator-focalizer (NF), while the internal focalizer will usually be a character-focalizer (CF). We need the cautious 'usually' here because of the fact that *external* and *internal* are entirely relative terms, since any particular focalization, as we shall see, can (like narration) be contained or embedded within another. So, for example, the narrator-focalizer of a hypodiegetic narrative may function simultaneously as external narrator-focalizer with regard to the story he or she narrates, and as internal character-focalizer with regard to the story in which he or she is a character.[4] Focalization, moreover, need not be constant throughout a text: indeed, it can be variable to any degree. Rimmon-Kenan thus makes a threefold distinction between *fixed* focalization, where the same focalizer is maintained throughout a narrative; *variable* focalization, employing, say, two different character-focalizers; and *multiple* focalization, employing several different types of focalization, internal or external or both (1983: 76–7).

Rimmon-Kenan makes the further valuable point that while focalization is always a matter of 'seeing,' the vision involved is by no means limited to physical vision, but can also include psychological and/or ideological components (77–82). The question

'Who sees?' should therefore be understood as potentially meaning 'Who perceives, conceives, assumes, understands, desires, remembers, dreams?' and so on. Each of these visions will have its separate implications for the kind of focalizer employed – and for the kind of reading we feel appropriate. We are unsurprised when an external narrator-focalizer is assigned a bird's-eye view in terms of space and a panchronic view of both past and future in terms of time, while we expect a character-focalizer to be 'naturally' confined to both a limited spatial perspective and a purely retrospective temporal vision. We readily accept that an external focalizer, like an external narrator, should lay claim to unrestricted knowledge, but assume that a character-focalizer's knowledge will be 'naturally' restricted, like our own. We tend to treat a character-focalizer's perspective cautiously as being subjective, but quite happily accept an external focalizer's vision as entirely objective. As in the case of the narrative voice, indeed, we tend to read the norms of internal focalization as questionable, those of external focalization as authoritative. Since externality and internality are interchangeable, however, the textual potential for manipulation of the reader here is abundantly evident.

Focalization, however, involves not only a subject of focalization, or focalizer; it also crucially involves an object of focalization, the *focalized*. In a sentence like 'John watched the train arriving,' the character-focalizer is 'John,' and 'the train' is the focalized, the object of John's attention. In the case of a novel like *Vanity Fair*, indeed, with its external narrator-focalizer who focalizes the entire narration, it is evident that *everything* in that narrative is focalized, whether or not there is *also* a character-focalizer involved at any given point. It is crucial to remember, however, that every narrative is created by a narrative voice that is by definition external to it. It follows that in *every* narrative *everything* is *primarily* focalized by this world-creating narrative agent, including all subsequent focalizations within that particular narrative world.

'Everything' includes both events and what Chatman calls 'existents,' namely, characters and setting (1978: 26). Characters as objects of focalization (CO) are particularly interesting in that

they can be focalized either 'from without' or 'from within,' to
employ Rimmon-Kenan's terms (75): that is to say, 'seen' by the
focalizer 'from without' as impenetrable, non-transparent, opaque
objects to be viewed from the outside only, like any other object;
or, alternatively, 'seen' by the focalizer 'from within,' as if the focalizer
could read their mind, could see 'through' them as transparent
rather than opaque objects. In the former case, the focalizer's
vision simply registers the focalized with whatever degree of
objectivity or subjectivity; in the latter case, however, the focalizer's
vision can be (though it *need* not be) transmuted to a greater or
lesser extent into the vision of the focalized, which consequently,
and correspondingly, becomes a focalizer in its turn – a transformation, incidentally, that has remained largely undiscussed among
narrative theorists.

Combined with the fact that focalization can be either internal
or external, this potential transformation of focalized and focalizer
provides a whole series of new perspectives. Thus, in a sentence
like 'John watched Mary,' for example, 'Mary' is a non-transparent character-focalized. In a sentence like 'John watched Mary,
who wished he would stop,' 'Mary' is still a non-transparent
focalized as far as the internal focalization by 'John' is concerned,
but in terms of focalization by the external *narrator* of the sentence as a whole, 'Mary' is a transparent focalized, since the
narrator, unlike John, can see 'through' her and her own focalization of the situation as an independent character-focalizer. In a
sentence like 'John could still see himself as a schoolboy, wishing
the summer would never end,' the older 'John' is a character-
focalizer, while the younger, remembered self is both a transparent character-focalized, and, with his wish that summer would
never end, also a secondary character-focalizer (CF2) *within* the
primary character-focalization (CF1) of his remembering, or fan-
tasizing, or self-deluding older self. That older self, in turn, is also
envisioned, namely as a projection of the *narrator* of the sentence
as global external focalizer (EF). The implications of this multiple
embeddedness of different focalizations have not yet been adequately theorized and will consequently be our central focus for
the remainder of this chapter.

As a final aspect of focalization that needs to be borne in mind before proceeding any further, however, we may, as Mieke Bal observes (1985: 109), mention the implications of the *perceptibility* or otherwise both of the focalizer and of the focalized. An external narrator-focalizer, for example, may just be a narrating voice that gives us an apparently entirely objective account of the events narrated but provides no information as to the personal identity of its owner, who thus, as focalizer, is non-perceptible; a narrator who gives his name and the circumstances surrounding his narration, on the other hand, is perceptible. It will be clear that such perceptibility or otherwise can involve increased or decreased authority for the narrator-focalizer: the more perceptible the focalizer becomes, and thus the more easily graspable as a character, the more the reader will in turn feel authorized to question the focalizer's vision. Bal points likewise to the perceptibility or non-perceptibility of the focalized object as being of importance especially as to the extent to which it can provide an insight into the power structure between focalizers (1985: 109). We are hardly surprised at all as readers when an external focalizer can focalize such non-perceptible objects as a character's thoughts or the contents of his dreams. We should no doubt be disturbed, on the other hand, if a character-focalizer focalized anything other than perceptible objects. In this respect, too, the potential for textual manipulation of the reader through focalization will be evident.

LEVELS OF FOCALIZATION

We may theoretically and provisionally (or *sous rature*, to use a fashionable Derrideanism) distinguish three possible levels of focalization – simple, compound, and complex – each of which may be seen as applying globally (that is, to whole texts) or regionally (to parts of texts). We can thus appropriately speak of *simple* focalization when there is only a single focalizer involved; we can speak of *compound* focalization when there is more than one focalizer involved, as when a character-focalizer's vision is embedded in an external focalizer's enveloping perspective; and we can speak of *complex* focalization in cases where the focalization is essentially ambiguous or indeterminate. It should be said at once, however, that the theory in this area, which is of considerable interest, is frequently a great deal clearer than the narrative practice, which consequently is even more interesting. Both the 'simple' and the 'compound,' in fact, as we shall see, demonstrate a pronounced tendency to slide systemically and irresistibly towards the complex.

Simple focalization, involving a single focalizer, can be said (provisionally) to occur when, for example, a single narrator also functions as focalizer for the entire duration of the text under consideration. In practice, however, this is rarely encountered in texts of more than a few sentences in length. One could also speak of simple focalization even in the case of multiple narrators, as long as each individual narrator functioned sequentially as sole focalizer for the duration of that portion of the text under consideration. It should, however, be noted that simple focalization is, in principle, limited to narrator-focalizers – and that, as we shall eventually see, also only provisionally – while character-focalization is always compound.

Compound focalization always involves, whether explicitly or implicitly, some form of embedded focalization, where one focalization is contained within another. We especially need to remember in this context that *the narrator is always a focalizer*, having no choice *whether* to focalize or not (just as he/she/it has no choice whether to verbalize or not), only *how* to do so. The narrator, in other words, necessarily has a particular 'vision' of the narrative world he/she/it projects.[5] As we have seen, the narrator may focalize objects directly or may choose to focalize them indirectly through one or more interposed character-focalizers. Focalization by a character is therefore always, of necessity, contained within an enveloping narrator-focalization and is consequently, in principle, always compound rather than simple. In practice, one could, for convenience' sake, choose to regard texts where a single character-focalization both remained constant and did not at any point yield the foreground to an external narrator-focalization as being *de facto* simple focalization. In theory, however, *de jure*, all character-focalization is compound – and it is thus, strictly speaking, always more appropriate to speak of focalization *through* a character rather than *by* a character.

This relationship can be formulated – since the use of schematic formulations may be helpful from this point on – as

$$F = (EF1 \, (CF2)).$$

Here F stands for the focalization under analysis, while EF1 indicates the primary and CF2 the secondary or embedded focalization.[6] There are many different forms of compound focalization. Objects can be focalized identically by (through) multiple characters simultaneously, for example, as when Robyn Penrose and Bob Busby 'turn to face Philip Swallow, who has evidently just arrived, since he is wearing his rather grubby anorak and carrying a battered briefcase' in David Lodge's *Nice Work* (61). Since the overall context provides no clue as to individual focalization here (even though Robyn Penrose is one of the two major focalizers in the text), the implication is that what is 'evidently' the case here is evident to any reasonable observer, in this case both of them at once. This could be formulated as

$$F = (EF1 \, (CF2_{Robyn} + CF2_{Bob} \rightarrow CO_{Philip})).$$

Here the focalizer and character-focalized (CO) are specified in subscript and the arrow indicates the action of focalization. Likewise, objects can be focalized simultaneously but differently by multiple characters, as when, in Beckett's *Watt*, we catch our first glimpse of Watt through the combined eyes of three evening strollers:

Tetty was not sure whether it was a man or a woman. Mr Hackett was not sure that it was not a parcel ... Goff [whom Watt turns out to have owed five shillings for the past seven years] rose, without a word, and rapidly crossed the street. (16–17)

Frequently, of course, the subject of focalization can switch abruptly from a character to a narrator – as it does in the example just cited from *Watt*, where Tetty and Mr Hackett function as embedded secondary focalizers, but Goff, though obviously also seeing Watt, is presented not as a focalizer but as a direct object of the narrator's own primary focalization. Such alternation between character-focalization and narrator-focalization, indeed, is entirely common, especially in narratives with a so-called omniscient narrator, as in *Wuthering Heights*:

'I shall not be at peace,' moaned Catherine [EF], recalled to a sense of physical weakness by the violent, unequal throbbing of her heart [(EF (CF$_{Catherine}$))], which beat visibly and audibly under this excess of agitation [EF]. (142)[7]

Likewise, to take a very much older example, in the Bible: Jesus 'entered into an house [EF], and would have no man know it [(EF (CF$_{Jesus}$))]; but he could not be hid [EF]' (Mark 7: 24).

So far we have been operating as if tacitly assuming that internal and external focalization were always clearly distinguishable, as if character-focalizers and narrator-focalizers could always and unproblematically be told apart. Such is by no means the case, however. Focalization need not be clearly identifiable and frequently *is* not, and such cases, as Rimmon-Kenan rightly observes, are almost always the most interesting ones (1983: 84). We shall refer to this kind of focalization as *complex* (as opposed to compound), in the sense that it provides us simultaneously with too much and too little information to make a definite decision as to the location of the focalizer. To this extent, complex focalization is essentially characterized by indeterminacy.

One writer whose narratives gain much of their pervasively enigmatic character from a sustained and masterly use of indeterminate focalization is Franz Kafka. The opening sentence of *The Trial* (1925), for example, initially reads as if it were an uncomplicated narrator-focalization: 'Someone must have traduced Joseph K., for without having done anything wrong he was arrested one fine morning' (1). Indeed, there is no technical reason why this should *not* be regarded as narrator-focalization pure and simple. 'Someone *must have* traduced' *could* simply be an assumption made by a character-narrator realistically aware of his incomplete control of all the facts, as could the further statement that Joseph K. was arrested 'without having done anything wrong.' As sentence follows sentence, however, the cumulative effect is to cause the reader to wonder if even the opening sentence should not retrospectively be read as character-focalization (by K.) after all:

His landlady's cook, who always brought him his breakfast at eight o'clock [EF? CF?], failed to appear on this occasion [more likely EF?]. That had never happened before [more likely CF?]. K. waited for a little while longer [EF?], watching from his pillow [more likely CF?] the old lady opposite, who seemed [CF] to be peering at him with a curiosity unusual even for her [CF], but then, feeling [CF] both put out and hungry, he rang the bell [EF]. (1)

Even though the reader's initial assumption of narrator-focalization may be unsettled by this sequence, however, he or she is still not provided at any stage with *unambiguous* evidence that that first reading was either right or wrong. The entire novel is characterized by this indeterminacy of focalization – as indeed are almost all of Kafka's other narratives.

It would be over-hasty to assume that such determined indeterminacy can be characterized as merely a product of the epistemological obsessions of high modernism, however, and as such constituting a relatively limited phenomenon. We find the following passage in Balzac's *Père Goriot* (1834), for example, which certainly contains its share of indeterminacy as far as focalization is concerned:

He [Vautrin] knew, or had guessed, the secrets of everyone in the place [EF? CF$_{Vautrin}$?]; his own thoughts and activities no one could fathom [EF? CF?] ... He evidently bore some deep-rooted grudge against the social order [Evident to whom? the no longer omniscient narrator? some other character?]; and somewhere in his life there was a carefully shrouded mystery [EF? CF$_{not-Vautrin}$?]. (20)

As for the other boarders of the Maison Vauquer, 'they all knew they were powerless to help one another' (20), which again can be read either as an omniscient narrator-focalization (EF → CO, the latter multiple and transparent) or a simultaneous embedded focalization by (or through) multiple focalizers.

Some readers might be rather more surprised to find indeterminate focalization even in the Bible. The object of biblical translation is certainly to convey the unadulterated meaning of the original text, seen traditionally as the very word of God himself, as completely accurately as possible. Yet, to take just one example, no less an authority than the Authorized Version changes the focalization of the last sentence of Mark 6: 48's original Greek quite radically – arguably producing a superior literary text in the process, but only at the semantic cost of allowing new and extra readings not catered for in the original text. The passage in question is a particularly interesting example, in that it reports one of the miracles performed by Jesus and displays an intriguing complexity of focalization in doing so:

And he saw them toiling in rowing [CF_{Jesus}]; for the wind was contrary unto them [EF]: and about the fourth watch of the night he cometh unto them [EF? $CF_{disciples}$?], walking upon the sea [EF? $CF_{disciples}$?], and would have passed by them [EF? $CF_{disciples}$? CF_{Jesus}?]. (Mark 6: 48)

The more ambiguous the focalization, of course, the more scope there is for interpretation. It is therefore especially interesting to observe what different Bible translations have made of the most complexly focalized phrase here, where Jesus 'would have passed by' the disciples in the boat. The original Greek is 'kai ēthelen parelthein autous'; the standard Latin translation has 'et volebat praeterire eos'; the Revised Standard Version has 'He meant to pass by them'; and a recent translation by E.V. Rieu has 'with the intention of passing them' (16) – all of which can be read either as externally focalized by an omniscient narrator or with Jesus as an embedded character-focalizer. The New International Version, however, has 'He was about to pass them by,' which also allows either of these possibilities – but also, and more emphatically, the possibility of the watching disciples as a multiple character-focalizer. The Authorized Version, as we have seen, with its 'and would have passed by them' goes furthest in allowing all three interpretations without emphasizing any of the three – which could certainly be read as a rather striking indeterminacy concerning a crucial event in the tradition and dogma of the Christian church.

The point here is not which of the translations is more accurate or more faithful to the original, but rather what reading each permits purely in terms of focalization. Certain lexical items, of course, have a built-in ambiguity. The effect of this on focalization in translation can be very significant. The biblical Greek *prospoieomai*, for example, 'to act as if, to give the impression that' implicitly contains the possibility of a dual character-focalization: by both the character who gives the particular impression and the character who receives it. Thus Luke 24: 28, 'kai autos *prosepoiēsato* porrōteron poreuesthai,' is translated in the Latin as 'et ipse *se finxit* longius ire,' and by E.V. Rieu as 'Jesus *gave them to understand* that he was going on,' where both translators opt for Jesus as character-focalizer. The Revised Standard Version, however, prefers 'He *appeared* to be going further,' where the focalization is unambiguously by the disciples rather than by Jesus. Both the Authorized Version ('and he *made as though* he would have gone further') and the New International Version ('Jesus *acted as if* he were going further'), like the Greek, allow both Jesus and the disciples as possible character-focalizers and thus permit an interpretive ambiguity not allowed by any of the other versions. Finally, of course, since all character-focalization is embedded, each of these versions also allows the alternative possibility of an external narrator-focalizer.

FOCALIZATION AND THE IMPLIED AUTHOR

Focalization is very evidently a phenomenon of discourse rather than story. But should it be located more specifically on the level of *text* or on that of *narration*? To some extent we can actually have our cake and eat it too in situating focalization on either level, depending on our purpose. For the obvious answer, in terms of the axiom that text is to narration as *how* is to *who*, would seem to be that we will locate focalization on the level of the narrative text if we see the primary question concerning it as being one of *how* focalization operates. If we see the primary question as being one of *who* – which is to say, which narrative agent – is ultimately responsible for the most authoritative level of focalization, then we will want to locate it on the level of narration. This, however, means situating the ultimate locus of focalization on the level of the *implied author* rather than the narrator, who is seen by most narrative theorists as the primary, which is to say, the most authoritative focalizer.

Most narratologists, indeed, have completely ignored the implied author in the discussion of focalization. In spite of such theorists as Bal and Rimmon-Kenan, however, who situate focalization on the level of text (the *product* of narration), there are very strong reasons for seeing it rather as part of the (inferred) *process* of narration itself.[8] Focalization, indeed, can be read as logically prior to the *act* of narration: before the narrative voice speaks, it is *positioned* (by the implied author) in time and space, a decision is made as to where (and when) the (implied) *reader* will position the point of origin of both the narrative voice and the primary focalization. To this extent focalization provides a bridge to the consideration of an area considered by classical narratology to be beyond the boundaries of its proper concern, namely extratextual textuality – a bridge that will become quite apparent in the final section of this chapter in the discussion of the role of contextual restraints in identifying focalization.

In so far as it can have a very major impact on the way the reader perceives the narrative world presented, focalization is clearly a powerfully manipulative textual device. A character who is also a focalizer has a special claim not only on readers' attention but also on their sympathy, for, as Bal observes, in such a case 'the reader watches with the character's eyes and will, in principle, be inclined to accept the vision presented by that character' (Bal 1985: 104). Likewise, when the focalization is external, the reader tends to accept it as being a purely 'objective' vision of the narrative world presented, in that it is *not* presented from the viewpoint of any one of the characters.

That assumed objectivity, however, is fundamentally questionable. Character-focalization, it was argued above, is in principle unreliable because it is always an embedded and therefore always an 'invented' focalization. To what extent, however, we now need to enquire, is an external narrator-focalizer ever entirely reliable either? If character-focalizers can always be presented in lights that suit the narrative agenda of their narrator, is the same not always in principle equally true of the narrator, however apparently objective, in so far as the narrator can be seen as merely a presentation of the verbalizing aspect of the implied author? An unreliable narrator, as Chatman observes (1978: 149), is evaluated as such by comparison with the implied author, who is the only unquestionable authority in the text that constitutes him/her/it. Likewise, a text may well have several external narrators, but by definition each text can have only a single implied author. It must in principle follow that all narrators are therefore *at least potentially* not only unreliable narrators but also unreliable focalizers. *Everything*, it likewise follows, is therefore ultimately – or rather, *primarily* – focalized by the implied author, through the interposed lens of the narrator(s), and possibly also through the further lens of one or more characters. The reader, however, is always fully aware only of the most *recent* focalization and is consequently almost entirely unaware throughout of the most important focalizer, the implied author, except, for example, in titles, chapter headings, and like paratextual information. Such information can, of course, be of central importance to our reading of the narrative. The fact that a novel is called *David Copperfield*, *Madame Bovary*, or *Anna Karenina* constitutes a crucial if minimal opening statement of the implied authorial focalization.[9]

We may detect further faint evidence of implied authorial focalization in a case such as the following, where the character-focalizer's perceptions and the narrator's voice seem to be not quite in harmony. In David Lodge's *Small World* (1984), Cheryl Summerbee, a British Airways check-in clerk with a talent for matchmaking, considers and decides where would be the best location for seating a particularly likable passenger: 'About a quarter of an hour ago she had dealt with an extremely elegant Italian lady professor, of about the right age – younger, but not too young – and who spoke very good English, apart from a little trouble with her aspirates' (116). Up until the very last word here the focalization, though clearly compound, is tilted so that we are much more aware of the character Cheryl than we are of the faceless narrator; since Cheryl is fairly unlikely to know what an 'aspirate' is, however, while the scholarly narrator certainly does, the use of that term effectively introduces an unexpected element of irony into the situation, as the external focalization gains the upper hand after all, revealing the compound focalization as, at least potentially, *dissonant* as opposed to *consonant*. Admittedly, it might well be objected that it would be less unnecessarily complicated to regard this simply as an example of irony on the part of the *narrator*, with no need to drag the implied author into it. Let us consider a further example before deciding.

Ben Watterson's widely read syndicated comic strip *Calvin and Hobbes* derives its comic effects very largely from a highly sophisticated use of focalization. The small boy Calvin's constant companion in triumph and adversity is Hobbes the tiger, who is at once the bane of Calvin's life, continually pouncing on him to devastating effect from one ambush or another, and his best friend and fellow participant in a series of escapades. Every frame of the cartoon where Calvin and Hobbes are alone together portrays Hobbes as a real tiger, and, depending on whether Calvin sees Hobbes as friend or foe, the subject of focalization is either Calvin-as-best-friend or Calvin-as-terrified-victim. In frames where anyone else is present, however, Hobbes is invariably portrayed as a stuffed toy. The subject point of focalization, that is to say, changes from the character Calvin to any character other than Calvin. In addition, we frequently encounter focalization that is overtly compound rather than ostensibly simple, for Hobbes often reacts to Calvin's madcap schemes and stratagems with a distinctly adult sense of irony, attributable neither to a small boy nor to a tiger (whether real or stuffed) and consequently inviting the reader to read it as a character-focalization, via Hobbes, overtly embedded in an external narrator-focalization, or

$$F = (EF (CF_{Hobbes} \rightarrow CO_{Calvin})).$$

There is a clearly a further level of focalization at play in *Calvin and Hobbes*, however, for finally there is the crucial point – so obvious as to be almost entirely invisible – that the whole thing is a comic strip, where the nature of the reality presented is quite different from that of the world the reader lives in: all of the characters are drawn precisely as *cartoon* characters, so Calvin, for example, will have three fingers on each hand in one frame, four in the next, his eyes literally come out on stalks when he is surprised, visible stars appear when he falls on his head, and so on through the usual gamut of graphic devices characteristic of comic strips. In other words, everything in this represented world is very overtly *as if*, and *all* the forms of focalization mentioned so far are in consequence further embedded, but *covertly* rather than overtly, in a global external focalization that takes precedence over all others.

This last type of focalization, however, is clearly not limited to *Calvin and Hobbes*, since the same argument could evidently be made for any comic strip. Indeed the extended argument can clearly be made that the overtly non-realist presentation of a narrative world typical of comic strips is different only in degree rather than in kind from *any* narrative presentation, however ostensibly realist that presentation may be. Comic-strip presentation is only one particular form of narrative discourse, and there can be no narrative without discourse. This, in turn, evidently implies that a *covert global external focalization* as suggested here is characteristic not just of cartoons but of *all* narrative texts. Clearly, we need a way of distinguishing this form of *covert* external focalization typical of *all* narratives from the *overt* external focalization we encounter in *some* narratives. The most economical (as well as the most aesthetically pleasing) way to achieve this end is to regard the former as focalized by the implied author rather than by the narrator. What we have been calling external focalization (EF) so far, in other words, emerges as being itself already a compound focalization, where the explicit perspective of an external narrator (ENF) is embedded in the implicit perspective of the implied author (A'F). Calvin as object of Hobbes's irony is thus the object of focalization in a situation that can be formulated more accurately and more completely as

$$F = (A'F1 \ (ENF2 \ (CF3_{Hobbes} \rightarrow CO_{Calvin}))).$$

It will be evident from all of this that ultimately all focalization tends towards the complex and indeterminate. The concept of 'simple' focalization, it emerges, is nothing more than a convenient (if useful) oversimplification: we were obliged first to disqualify character-focalization as simple; now it is evident that narrator-focalization cannot be simple either, since it, too, is embedded; and even the ultimate focalization, that of the implied author, can finally be expressed only through the voice of the narrator – and likewise becomes questionable in the process. All focalization, it emerges, is always compound – but because of the multiple layers of overlapping and intersecting visions involved, *compound* must always, as far as the reader is concerned, be just another word for *complex*.

Meanwhile, what *of* the reader? If there is an implied authorial focalization, to what extent must there also be an implied *readerly* focalization? We can profitably turn at this point to a concluding consideration of the role of the reader, both implied and real, as an 'agent' of focalization in the very practical sense that the reader, after all, finally has to *decide* which of these multiple complications need to be seen as more important and which can afford to be discounted or even disregarded, at least provisionally.

FOCALIZATION AND CONTEXTUALITY

If complex or indeterminate focalization, far from being an exotic or unique occurrence, is in principle the *only* kind of focalization we encounter as readers, then the narrative terrain is, in principle, *always* strewn with potential unadvertised detours and misleading signposts. Many of the most effective tricks of focalization employed by the text in throwing the reader at least momentarily off balance are often surprisingly inconspicuous. Simple pronouns, for example, can have a disproportionately significant effect on our perception of focalization. Take a passage like the following:

Now he was in the midst of the sheep, they made a circle round him, their eyes converged on him. Perhaps he was the butcher come to make his choice.

There is no particular problem in describing the focalization here: the focalizer in the first sentence is either the narrator (EF) or the embedded character-focalizer 'he'; the second ('Perhaps he was the butcher ...') involves an embedded focalization whose object is 'he,' either a somewhat unlikely

$$F = (EF \ (CF_{sheep} \rightarrow CO_{he}))$$

or, more likely, the doubly embedded

$$F = (EF \ (CF1_{he} \ (CF2_{sheep} \rightarrow CO_{he}))).$$

In Beckett's *Molloy*, however, the passage actually occurs with first-person rather than third-person pronouns:

Now I was in the midst of the sheep, they made a circle round me, their eyes converged on me. Perhaps I was the butcher come to make his choice. (159)

The basic focalization is unchanged, with the substitution of 'I' for 'he' – including in the second sentence, where 'I' rather than 'he' is now the object of focalization. The powerful sense of dislocation engendered by having 'I' function as the object rather than the immediate subject of focalization in a first-person (or homodiegetic) narration, however, demonstrates the surprising effectiveness of what in itself is a relatively simple stylistic device.

Clearly, however, in spite of such allegedly pervasive indeterminacy, we do not in practice usually allow ourselves as readers to be entirely becalmed by proliferating visions of interpretive entropy. But how do we actually go about establishing the most appropriate focalization, since, as practical readers rather than focalization theorists, that is exactly what we have to do? In practical terms, the answer is clear – and comfortingly pragmatic: we will choose whichever particular reading seems most warranted by our overall reading of the situation as a whole, by our perception, that is to say, of the overall *context* involved. That perceived context, in turn, will be established by our notions of overall interpretive *relevance*.

A contextually unacceptable character-focalization will thus, for instance, usually be read as *implying* a different focalization, namely one that is more acceptable in terms of the reader's perception and expectations of the overall narrative and interpretive context. An interesting example of this can be found in Elizabeth George's detective novel *A Great Deliverance* (1988), where the child Bridie is feeding her pet duck as she talks to Inspector Thomas Lynley:

She hopped off the steps and filled a shallow pan with water. 'Here, Dougal,' she called. The duck ignored her. There was a chance the food might be taken away if he did not eat it all as fast as he could. Dougal was a duck who never took chances. Water could wait. Bridie rejoined Lynley. Companionably, they watched as the duck gorged himself. (183)

Here the character-focalization in sentences 4 to 6, though ostensibly that of Dougal the duck, is hardly likely to be attributable primarily to the consciousness of a barnyard fowl, since this particular narrative world is predicated on realistic assumptions rather than the assumptions of, say, a child's story like Beatrix Potter's *Tale of Jemima Puddleduck*, where such reflective cerebration on the part of a duck would be entirely acceptable. Since Dougal as focalizer,

$$F = (EF\ (CF_{Dougal})),$$

would therefore attribute a whimsicality to the narrator that is otherwise nowhere in evidence (and would consequently be entirely pointless in the context of this narrative world), we are led – as in the case of Molloy's sheep – to assume a further embedding, namely

$$F = (EF (CF1 (CF2_{Dougal}))).$$

Since CF1 could be either Lynley or Bridie or even both simultaneously, how do we then go about the next step of deciding whether the focalization is indeterminate or localizable? It is clear that the decision will again rest on the narrative context, and essentially that means on grounds of perceived narrative relevance. Thus, to begin with, our generic expectations remind us that a localizable rather than an indeterminate focalization is far more *likely* in what up to this point has been a work of detective fiction in the classic tradition. Likewise, our expectations of realist fiction remind us that the focalization is fairly unlikely to be a product of Bridie's uncomplicated eight-year-old consciousness. More important, the episode would again lack a narrative point even if the focalization *were* attributable to Bridie. It is, however, entirely consonant with what we know of the thought processes of the aristocratic and intellectual Inspector Lynley – an engaging blend of Adam Dalgliesh and Lord Peter Wimsey – so the most likely (which means, the most globally persuasive) reading in this particular narrative context is clearly a doubled embedded character-focalization, namely

$$F = (EF (CF1_{Lynley} (CF2_{Dougal}))).$$

The reader, in other words, processes the information as one more factor in the continuing characterization of Lynley, which is a central point of this particular narrative and therefore has a very high narrative relevance. The fact that 'EF' is 'really' '(A'F (ENF)),' on the other hand, has no relevance whatsoever to the reader's immediate interpretive problem here, and can consequently be completely ignored – as it certainly would *not*, however, in the case of a contextually appropriate reading of an overtly self-interrogative, self-parodic detective fiction like Robbe-Grillet's *Le Voyeur* (1955), where the narrative point is less the presentation of believable characters than the presentation of narrative presentation itself.

Contextual relevance is also the yardstick we routinely employ as readers in deciding to what degree we should ignore the fundamental – if to date largely disregarded – axiom that all character-focalization is already embedded. The reason why we should be interested in doing this in the first place, we recall, is that character-focalization is in principle *always unreliable*, since it is made available to the reader only through the mediation of a prior focalization, namely that of the narrator, whose words constitute the only textual level to which we have unmediated access. One can therefore, in principle, never say with certainty that any example of focalization *is* a character-focalization, but only that it is *presented* as such by a narrator who in turn may or may not be reliable. Should we ignore this, however, in practice if not in theory? Especially when watching, say, a theatre performance, where the theoretically present narrator is only minimally in evidence?

Again, it is the context of how we think we are *supposed* to behave as readers that ultimately decides for us. As spectators of a theatre performance, our natural tendency is certainly to identify with the characters we see living out their lives before us, strangely unaware of our presence. Even the most hardened movie-goer or reader of romantic fiction will occasionally wipe away a stealthy tear or have his heart skip a reluctant beat over the lot of a vividly experienced character. Within this psychological context the reader/viewer is certainly *experiencing* an entirely unmediated character focalization, to the degree that he or she has been drawn into the narrative inhabited by the character. In a theoretical context, however, it is clear that the distinction between dramatic or filmic narrative and literary narrative in the narrower sense is entirely a matter of degree rather than kind. However unnoticed the external focalization embedding the character-focalization may be, in other words, its existence is no less true – but only in theory. In practice, as readers, we very happily (and very properly) ignore it.

Different kinds of writing, in fact, have quite different general 'requirements' – of both authors and readers – as to the kinds of focalization deemed appropriate. Non-fictional narrative, not surprisingly, tends to favour the most authoritative focalization, namely external. More interestingly, even though character-focalization is quite possible in perfectly professional historical narratives, we will *read* it quite differently than we would if we knew we were reading a work of fiction instead. Thus in E.J. Passant's *Short History of Germany*, the scholarly narrator informs us at one point that the Kaiser's 'determination to build a great navy involved the alienation of Great Britain, yet he had no real desire to fight this – or indeed any other – country' (122). The degree to which the context of reading determines the perceived focalization now becomes very apparent. For if this were a fictional text, we would most likely simply accept this as an embedded character-focalization reflecting the conventional ability of a traditional omniscient narrator to read his characters' thoughts and intentions, and we would read the primary relevance of the device as being the development of the fictional character. Since such a reading would clearly be inappropriate to a modern work of historical scholarship, however, we regard the equally embedded character-focalization here as meaning something like 'Having soberly reviewed all the evidence available to me, I must conclude as narrator that the Kaiser had no real desire to fight' – where the emphasis shifts to the reliability of the *account*, to the discourse, in fact, rather than the characters presented in the story told. In the same work there is a reference to a discussion between Hindenburg and his adviser Papen as to how best Hitler might be kept under control in early 1933: 'Papen had an alternative plan. Hitler was now in a more humble mood. Had not the time come to make him Chancellor, but a Chancellor in chains?' (183). Again the (context-determined) implication is that the *narrator* proposes a particular motive for Hindenburg's later decision to offer Hitler the chancellorship of the Weimar Republic. In the quite different context of a work of fiction, we would read exactly the same focalization as once again being primarily relevant to the characterization of Papen.

The essential issue that focalization theory attempts to address, as Michael Toolan writes, is certainly that of *attribution* (1988: 75), of situating most appropriately the point of origin of the narrative vision presented. It will be evident, however, that in order to make that attribution in the most comprehensive terms, the reader needs to expand Genette's original heuristic 'Who sees?' (1980: 186) to the more broadly focused question 'Who, in what context, is presented as seeing?' It will also be abundantly evident that focalization is by no means just one more handy item in the narrator's bag of technical tricks, a rhetorical rabbit on the level of, say, analepsis or prolepsis, to be pulled out of the discursive hat only on special occasions when some particularly striking effect is needed. On the contrary, not only is focalization, implicitly or explicitly, *always* present in narrative, whether fictional or non-fictional, literary or non-literary; it is an absolutely crucial, entirely unavoidable, and fundamentally characteristic component of narrative as a discursive system. Pervading all narrative, its subversive potential, as will have become clear, is equally all-pervasive.

5

Texts and Textuality:
The Shapers and the Shaped

The model of narrative structure built up in the preceding chapters involves certain implications that can now be examined more closely. In this chapter we shall therefore turn first to some of the implications of the necessarily *embedded* status of narrative levels and discuss the degree to which these nested levels also constitute nested 'narrative worlds,' each deconstructively relativized by its 'parent' world embodied on and by the next higher narrative level. We shall then examine the usefulness of expanding the consciously more limited narratological concept of the text as product by including within the general narratological paradigm as employed so far in previous chapters appropriate consideration of post-structuralist 'textological' concepts of the text as process. In this expanded model of narrative structure the nesting of narrative levels and worlds is read as continuing beyond the strictly 'intratextual' confines of the text in the received narratological sense to the 'extratextual' realms of that textuality in which the entire narrative structure is always already embedded. The 'highest' level or world in this expanded structural model, grounded, as we shall see, in paradox, not only relativizes all 'lower' levels or worlds but is also self-deconstructive. This element of systemic metatextual play leading to a systemic self-relativization centrally characterizes the essentially ludic, self-ironizing nature of narrative as a semiotic structure.[1] In the present chapter, therefore, we shall be examining what one might call the final extension of the Zeno Principle: not only is narrative discourse always at least potentially subversive of the story it purports to reconstruct, as we have argued so far; it is also, always and already, inherently self-subversive as well.

THE PLAY OF DISCOURSE

The relationship between story, text, and narration is a paradoxical and ludic one. We know very well that Emma Bovary never existed and yet we tend intuitively, naïvely, to think of her *story* as being in some sense more real, more primary, than the particular narrative strategies employed to present it. And yet the text, the textual presentation, is all we have, in a very real sense: 'there is not, *first of all*, a given reality, and *afterward*, its representation by the text. The given is the literary text; starting from it, by a labor of *construction* ... we reach that universe where certain characters live, comparable to the persons we know "in life"' (Todorov 1981: 27). Likewise, it is also through the text, and only through the text, that we can acquire knowledge of the narration, namely knowledge of the process of its production. The relationship between both text and story, on the one hand, and text and narration, on the other, is a paradoxical one, however, for 'the narrative text is itself defined by these other two aspects: unless it told a story it would not be a narrative, and without being narrated or written it would not be a text' (Rimmon-Kenan 1983: 4). We may thus think of both story and narration as synecdochic abstractions from the concrete narrative text: just as characters 'really' exist on the level of story (which is, however, an abstraction), so narrative authority 'really' resides on the level of narration (which, however, is also an abstraction).

This ludic, metonymic, and paradoxical relationship of the levels of narration of the narrative text is reflected in the complex interrelationship of our narrative personalia and allows equally complex realization of the play potential of narrative as a discursive system. To speak of narrative personalia is, of course, merely a metaphor. Neither characters, narrators, narratees, nor implied authors or readers are real persons in any but a metaphorical sense: they are *narrative agents*, narrative instances, and the most

Real author	Implied author	Narrator	Charac- ters	Narratee	Implied reader	Real reader
(A	A′	N	C	N′	R′	R)

Figure 5.1 Narrative personalia

appropriate pronoun for each of them is essentially *it* rather than *he* or *she*, though it is, of course, convenient to refer to them, as I have been doing throughout, in anthropomorphic terms; however, this should be read as meaning that they are conceived of not *as* persons but *as if* they were persons.

A curtain call of these narrative personalia as identified in an earlier chapter would result in the arrangement shown in figure 5.1. Working outwards in concentric circles from the centre of our diagram of dramatis personae, we move from the level of characters to that of narrator and narratee. Every word in the text is 'spoken,' or, as in the case of directly reported speech, at least presented by the narrator, who, after all, might have chosen to omit such information. Similarly, however inconspicuous his presence, the narratee, as the semiotically necessary receiver of the narrator's discourse, is never absent, every word of the narrator's being intended for him (it) alone. Between them, these two agents construct the text that discourses the story of the characters, the narrator's discourse evoked by the presence of the narratee as receiver. Their relationship to the world of the characters is godlike, for, in view of the hierarchical relationship between the two levels, one negative word of the narrator would in principle, as we have seen, be sufficient to alter radically the entire meaning of the world of the story (Bal 1985: 149).

If the characters' relationship to the narrator of their story is indeed that of 'flies to wanton boys,' the narrator's freedom is by no means unlimited either: common sense reminds us that the narrator, too, is the fictional creation of an author. Indeed, the narrator is a fiction of a fiction, for between narrator and author there is one more narrative level, that of narration, constructed in this case by the implied author and his/her/its counterpart, the implied reader, the hypothetical reader perfectly attuned to every textual nuance woven into the narrative by the implied author. We never *see* or *hear* the implied author; we can only infer his presence informing the narrator's narration, for the only *voice* we ever hear is the narrator's. The implied author, in other words, situates the narrator with regard to the discourse delivered by the narrator.

On the hierarchical level immediately superior to that of the implied author and implied reader we finally encounter – on a level we may now refer to as that of *textuality* – the real author and the real reader, and we might be tempted to heave a sigh of relief at reaching solid ground again after the narrative parade of ghostly presences. The relief would be premature, however: the traditional notion of the objectively receptive reader unproblematically quaffing of the vessel of meaning previously and unproblematically poured full by a sovereign author has turned out to be as riddled with paradox as any other level of the narrative transaction. None of these levels is independent, each is metonymically constituted by its difference from its neighbours, just as its neighbours are in turn constituted by their difference from it. Even on the individual narrative levels the relationship between agent and message is determined by paradox: the narrator and narratee both constitute the text and are simultaneously constituted by it; the implied author and implied reader both determine the process of narration and are in turn determined by that narration; each of these agents, and the real author and reader as well, of course, can operate only through the medium of language – language whose wall-to-wall uncontrollability has become an axiomatic given for increasingly larger areas of literary theory.

In the light of this view of the narrative process, our curtain-call of narrative personages may be recast as a series of nested narrative levels, nested frames. Each of these narrative frames, moreover, can be said to constitute a *possible narrative world*. The notion of 'possible worlds' was first adumbrated by Leibniz in 1710, when he contended in the *Theodicy* that since God as an omnipotent being could have created an infinite number of possible worlds if he had wanted to, the one world he did choose to

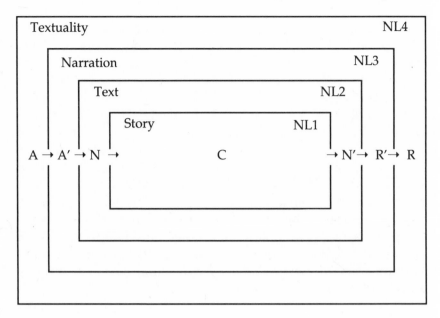

Figure 5.2 Narrative levels, narrative worlds

create, since he is also a being of infinite goodness, must be the very best world there could ever be, 'the best of all possible worlds' (1952: 128) – a phrase turned into a household word by Voltaire's determined rebuttal of Leibnizian optimism in *Candide*. The usefulness of the concept in modern semantic theory rests on the elegantly simple notion that when describing the hypothetical developments of a given situation, where any one of an indefinite number of possible states of affairs might at some point obtain, it is sometimes useful to think of individual states of affairs as constituting a 'possible world,' which may or may not coincide with the description of the actual world at some point (Lyons 1977: 163).[2] In these terms, our *narrationis personae* exist in a complex of nested possible worlds, which we might portray as in figure 5.2.

Each of our nested narrative frames or worlds could have been projected quite differently had the narrative agency of any one of the higher-ranked worlds so 'chosen' – but this 'choice' would

also have involved a chain reaction of differences in the superior
levels of the hierarchy as well. The controllers in the narrative
godgame, to use the term John Fowles introduced in *The Magus*
(cf. Wilson 1990: 144) are controlled by what they control. The
four narrative levels (NL) of our diagram represent only the tip
of the iceberg, however, as far as narrative complexity is concerned. The narrator, as we already know, may well focalize his
narrative through the eyes of one (or several) of the characters
rather than his own, for example, thus relativizing both his own
voice and their vision in a polyvocal act of narration, while characters themselves can also be narrators (and focalizers) *within* the
story and address their narratives to other characters who then
serve as narratees, and so on in a potentially infinite regress of
stories within stories, memorably exemplified in the following
bravura passage – one of many – from John Barth's *Lost in the
Funhouse* (1968):

'''''''''Speak!' Menelaus cried to Helen on the bridal bed," I reminded
Helen in her Trojan bedroom,' I confessed to Eidotheia on the beach," I
declared to Proteus in the cavemouth,' I vouchsafed to Helen on the
ship," I told Peisistratus at least in my Spartan hall,' I say to whoever
and where- I am. And Helen answered: '''''''''Love!''''''''' (150)

This, admittedly, is an extreme example. Potentially, however,
all narrative always involves a similar multiple play of levels and
metalevels. Recent metafictional narrative merely makes playfully overt what has always, of necessity, been narrative practice.
Characters act within the confines of their own world; narrators
observe from within the different confines of theirs. The character's
milieu is sequentiality, uncertainty, unpredictability; the narrator's
milieu, as far as his or her relationship to the world of that character is concerned, is arrangement, certainty, predictability. The
character operates on what Jakobson (1956) called the syntagmatic
or metonymic axis, the axis of syntax and 'just one damn thing
after another'; the narrator operates at right angles to this time-
bound world and privileges instead the paradigmatic or meta-
phoric axis, the axis of semantics and interpretation. Even if nar-

rative is conceived of simply as a two-level structure involving level and metalevel, story and its telling, it is still inevitably a ludic or play structure because of the element of discursive *choice* involved. Seen as a multilevelled structure involving not only a narrator but an implied author and a real author as well, together with their three receptive counterparts, the play potential increases exponentially, each of the narrative levels serving as a potentially subversive metalevel to the one immediately below it: the narrator's discourse is itself 'story' to the implied author's discourse, which is in turn 'story' to the authorial discourse. The complexity as well as the amount of the information transmitted and received increases at each higher level, the whole constituting not just a structure, but an interlocking structure of structures (cf. Barthes 1968: 89–94), which might be graphically represented as in figure 5.3.

In this system of nested narrative worlds there can be no absolutes, no certainties beyond revision. The agents on every level exist only to the extent that they are *discoursed* on a higher level as existing. If we adopt a simple system of notation to convey the suggestion of nested worlds, it is clear that a character (C) is thus never simply

$$C = (\,C\,),$$

i.e., a character existing in an absolute and unmediated world, but is always both

$$C = (\,N\,(\,C\,)),$$

i.e., the character as discoursed by the narrator (N), and

$$C = ((\,C\,)\,N'),$$

i.e., the character as received by the narratee (N'). Indeed, to be more accurate, the character is

$$C = (\,N\,((\,C\,))\,N'),$$

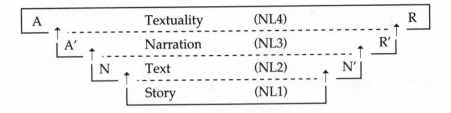

Figure 5.3 Nested narrative worlds

i.e., constituted *interactively* by the simultaneous discursive projection of one narrative agent and the discursive reception by another. Once we introduce the implied author (A′) and the implied reader (R′), our character metamorphoses into

$$C = (A' ((N ((C)) N')) R');$$

the introduction of the real author (A) and the real reader (R) involves seeing the character as

$$C = (A ((A' ((N ((C)) N')) R')) R);$$

and if we further regard both author and reader as inextricably embedded in the play of textuality (T′), a point to which we shall return, we finally obtain the entirely monstrous but usefully suggestive formula

$$C = (T' ((A ((A' ((N ((C)) N')) R')) R)) T').$$

While the naïve reader may see a character like Emma Bovary or Raskolnikov or David Copperfield as essentially a real person, in other words, the stability of that 'reality' quickly deconstructs when viewed in the light of narrative theory, revealing itself as a highly volatile, complex, and, above all, entirely provisional construct.

In the relationship between the worlds of the narrator and his or her characters, the narrator is all-powerful. Vladimir Nabokov's narrator in *Pnin* (1957) gives us a good example of the essential 'unfairness' of that relationship when he opens his account with a page-long description of the ageing, balding, and habitually bumbling Professor Pnin sitting contentedly in a train he confidently assumes is carrying him towards the university where he is supposed to give an invited lecture the same evening. After a page of this the narrator observes: 'Now a secret must be imparted. Professor Pnin was on the wrong train. He was unaware of it, and so was the conductor, already threading his way through the train to Pnin's coach' (8). Essentially, characters *never* know whether they are on the right or wrong train, and the narrator (once again as far as his relationship to that character is concerned) always knows. Nabokov – like García Márquez in the opening sentence of *One Hundred Years of Solitude* (1967), with its ostentatious employment of prolepsis – merely highlights what is an essential constant of the relationship between the character and the narrator.

One of the most interesting ludic effects deriving from the conception of nested narrative worlds is that of what Genette calls *metalepsis* (1980: 234), namely the illicit transgression of the boundaries of those worlds, when, for example, characters *do* 'escape' from their rightful narrative level to a higher one, as in Flann O'Brien's *At Swim-Two-Birds* (1939), where the 'author' character Dermot Trellis is tried while asleep by his own characters for alleged injustices perpetrated upon them. Such metalepses are frequently employed for comic effect, of course, and consequently occur regularly in more sophisticated comic strips. Thus one of Gary Larson's best *The Far Side* cartoons (which appeared in my local newspaper on 2 April 1990) shows a dejected office worker sitting at his desk with a 'thinks' balloon over his head reading 'Oh great, here comes my boss, that big, dumb, geek. I hate him so!' while the big dumb geek in question triumphantly retorts (as reported in a caption rather than in a speech-balloon), 'Oh yeah? Lewis, you're fired! You apparently forgot this is a cartoon, and I can read every word you think!' While such comic disruption of the 'reality' of the story-world presented tends to strike us as both exotic and ingenious, however, it is also worth remembering that completely non-comic disruption of story-reality is entirely commonplace (and usually entirely ignored) in such standard theatrical conventions as the missing fourth wall or everybody's failure to notice that Hamlet, inexplicably, speaks only in blank verse. Such an observation, however, brings us directly to the next topic to be considered, namely the matter of *textuality*.

DISCOURSE AND TEXTUALITY

At this point the time has come to recall (and exploit) the duality involved in the term *text*. While we have so far been using the term consistently in its strictly narratological sense as meaning the concrete product of the (metonymically inferred) act of narration, the 'words upon the page' and nothing else, it will now bear repeating that in post-structuralist usage the term *text* has come to have a far wider meaning. Roland Barthes, himself an eminent narratologist of impeccably structuralist provenance during the sixties, notoriously abandoned the confines of classical narratology for the headier realms of post-structuralist 'textology' in his masterpiece *S/Z* (1970), in which the 'text' is now seen as an ever changing intersection of multiple currents of shaping intentionality, both intratextual (as in classical narratology) *and* extratextual.[3] Traditional literary scholarship had always put a high premium on the extratextual level, of course, sometimes to the extent of seeing it as the *only* level of real interest. But where traditional scholarship sees authorial intention as the single admissible form of intentionality, one of Barthes's most liberating contributions consists in seeing textual intentionality as multidirectional (1974: 5). It is this continuing process of construction of the text on the extratextual level, reflecting *both* authorial *and* readerly intentionality as well as multiple forms of intentionality beyond the control of either authors or readers, that I shall now refer to as the level of *textuality*, which thus essentially asks the question 'What converts the (narratological) "text" as static product into the (post-structuralist) "text" as dynamic process?' – or, more simply, 'What enables the "same" text to mean different things to different readers?'

For narrative theorists trained in classical French narratology, it should be made clear, what I am calling 'textuality' here has nothing at all to do with the proper study of narrative *qua* narrative.[4] Such an objection is valid, however, only as long as we agree to regard the narrative transaction as being definitively concluded by the interaction of the implied author and the implied reader, to the exclusion of the real author, situated in a particular place, time, and culture, and the potentially innumerable real readers situated for the most part, perhaps, in very different places, times, and cultures. Theorists are, of course, perfectly entitled to limit the range of narrative theory to strictly intratextual concerns if they so choose. Much recent narrative theory, however, in its concern for the various historical, cultural, and ideological currents in which narrative texts are situated, finds it necessary to posit a much wider range of investigation, giving appropriate consideration to the multifarious extra-textual factors such as gender, race, and class that also go to shape the narrative text. To this extent the desirability of a formal model that can theoretically accommodate such concerns is clear. Whether they are literary or non-literary, fact or fiction, written or oral, narratives are never *simply* narratives: they are also *texts* in the post-structuralist sense. As soon as any story, however simple, *becomes* a story by being *told*, it also gives rise to a proliferation of possible intersecting meanings – or, as one might also put it, it enters the realm of textuality. Its narrativity, in other words, is a constituent part of its textuality – and thus cannot be adequately described by theoretical models that neglect an appropriate account of that textuality.

Textuality in this sense, the outermost box in our diagram of nested narrative levels (figure 5.2), concerns both the voluntary and the involuntary interactivity of authors, readers, and texts, and thus refers ultimately to the quality of *wovenness* of the literary text, a quality already signalled as central by the etymology of the term: Latin *textum*, 'that which is woven,' from *texere*, 'to weave, plait, construct.' Corresponding to the voluntariness or involuntariness of this relationship as far as authors and readers are concerned, we can furthermore see textuality itself as constituted by the interaction of two quite separate but inextricably interlinked processes, which we may refer to respectively as *metatextuality* and *intertextuality*. The former concerns a process of voluntary shaping, the latter one of being involuntarily shaped.[5]

In any process, we may speak of a *subject* who operates on a particular *object* or raw material and in so doing changes the object into the *product* of the process. In these terms, the process of metatextuality involves the author and each of his or her readers as individual subjects, the narratological text as object, and the transformation of that object-text into a *metatext*, a meaning-laden product both of the author's writing and of the reader's reading as dual and interactive shapers of the text. The text is necessarily and continually converted into ever new metatexts as the result of the interaction of this dual intentionality: on the one hand by that of its author, who necessarily intends his or her text to have a particular meaning or set of meanings by virtue of its particular qualities of wovenness, its quality of being a particular artefact, the product of skilled artifice; on the other by that of every reader who reads the text and naturally also intends it to have a particular meaning by virtue of his or her own particular reading of it – which may, of course, also differ significantly from any previous reading the 'same' reader may have undertaken of the 'same' text. Every reading, every interpretation, thus creates a new metatext – the difference between the object-text and its metatext being most graphically apparent in the case of translations.

Classical narratology, as we have seen, by and large regards the implied author and implied reader as legitimate objects of concern. On the level of textuality the real author and real reader become central objects of concern, not as real-world persons but precisely as being themselves texts – or, more specifically, as being intertexts. If the process of metatextuality involves the voluntary work of author and reader as shapers of metatexts, the process of intertextuality most essentially involves the involuntary processes by which that shaping is shaped, by which the author and the reader, not as subjects but as objects of the intertextual process, are themselves shaped, written, inscribed as characters in what Lyotard (1984: 34) has characterized as the intersecting 'metanarratives' of their time and place, namely the multiply interactive linguistic, anthropological, sociological, and psychological systems in and by which we are each assigned not always starring roles in particular but endlessly changing narrations of our existence. If the process of metatextuality involves authors and readers as voluntary subjects of reading and writing, the process of intertextuality involves them as involuntary objects of metanarrative inscription; if the product of metatextuality is to some extent characterizable as an at least temporary 'end'-product, namely the metatext produced by each individual act of reading or writing, the product of intertextuality can never be so characterized, for the essence of intertextuality is that its product is also always its object, must always continue to be changed, continue to be produced, continue to be an intertext. This is equally the case whether we are speaking primarily of the text as involuntarily processed or of the author and reader themselves as involuntarily shaped metatextual performers of acts of reading and writing.

Metatextuality and intertextuality are thus two inextricably interrelated aspects of textuality, two sides of the same textual coin, the text as shaped and the text as shapable. Metatext is to intertext as answer is to question, and since every answer always potentially invites further question, so every metatext is itself also an intertext requiring further metatextualization, further reading. Every individual act of reading (or writing) a text thus both creates a metatext and *is* an intertext, whose primary relevance is its situatedness, its betweenness, its provisionality, its further shapability, its further interpretability. Metatextuality is the necessary response to the centrally constitutive intertextual quality of the literary text that it always demands a reading (including the initial reading that is the author's writing), the quality of necessarily being woven and rewoven by an interactive process of authorial and readerly work. The literary text, by its nature, calls for an endless series – or better, an infinite network – of such always provisional metatexts, texts about texts, responses, interpretations, translations, workings, readings, rewritings. Every reading is thus a process of producing a new but always only provisional metatext, and in this sense the *full* meaning of the text must ultimately remain forever incomplete, must always and inevitably move towards the status of an unreachable supertext or macrotext, consisting of *all* possible readings, at all times, in all places. (We shall explore some of the interpretive possibilities of this concept in our next chapter).

The literary text is thus written by its author, rewritten by its readers, *inter*written by intertextual currents and tensions of which it is simultaneously a constituent part, as are its metatextual shapers, shaped themselves by the same cultural, historical, and ideological currents that enable them to shape the text. Intertextuality might thus be defined as the sum of all those *contextualizing* forces – such as our notions about literariness, canons, genres, periodization, for example, not to mention such extraliterary matters as history, culture, and ideology – that in effect *pre-read* the text for us as readers, just as they *pre-wrote* it for the author. Metatextuality is the process in which the author and the reader function as subjects of intentionality; intertextuality is the process in which the author and the reader, like the texts they shape, function themselves as texts, as *inter*texts, no longer subjects but simultaneously objects and products of an unceasing intertextual intentionality.

How, finally, must we view the relationship of 'textuality' and 'discourse' in such a context? At this point it will be evident that although we may have been telling the (narratological) truth about discourse in previous chapters, we have not been telling the whole (textological) truth. Discourse for narratologists means the *intratextual* discourse that shapes the telling and thus the meaning of the story told. But this is clearly not the whole story, for the meaning of a text continually changes as the context of its reception changes, and as that meaning changes so does the telling, for it is no longer the same story that is being told. The story,

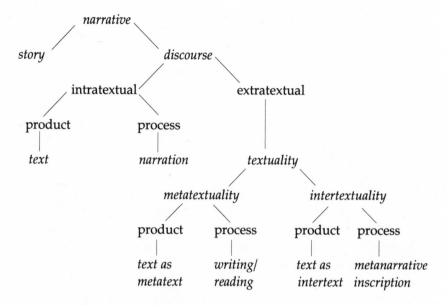

Figure 5.4 Discourse and textuality

that is, is shaped not just by the intratextual discourse that has traditionally been regarded as the proper domain of narratology (and to which we, too, have limited ourselvelves in previous chapters), but also and systemically by that *extratextual* discourse that we are calling textuality. Clearly, in other words, there is a sense in which the textuality of a text is also a *part* of its *discourse*, and that in turn means that we must see narrative discourse as operating both 'inside' and 'outside' the text. Our previous discussion of the relationship of narrative levels thus needs to be expanded and modified as portrayed in figure 5.4 if it is to tell the whole textological story, not just the narratological story, of how narrative discourse functions.

THE PLAY OF TEXTUALITY

What makes a text a text in the post-structuralist sense is the interaction of a process of construction on the part of an author and a process of construing on the part of a reader. There have been four major paradigms or models of reading employed in the critical discussion of literature during the twentieth century. We may characterize the four models in terms of intentionality, or, in other words, in terms of their different conceptions of where the ultimate seat of authority is to be found in the relationship of author, text, and reader. The first model is constituted by a traditional concern with the overriding primacy of authorial intention. For this model, the text means what it means because that is what its author intended it to mean, and any other meanings discovered by over-zealous readers are inadmissible, essentially on the grounds that such authorially unintended meanings are simply not 'there' and are read 'into' rather than 'out of' the authorially defined text. This is the position of traditional pre-formalist criticism. The second model is constituted by formalist concern with an assumed intentionality of 'the text itself,' independent of either author or reader. The third model is constituted by various versions of reader theory, stressing the constructive role of readerly rather than authorial intentionality, and the fourth model, our primary concern here, is constituted by the interest of semiotic and post-structuralist criticism in the communicative interactivity of authorial, textual, and readerly intentionality simultaneously, constituting what we can call a model of macrotextual interactivity, as we have seen.

The chronological sequence of these four paradigms of reading may be schematized in the formula

$$A \rightarrow T \rightarrow R \rightarrow (ATR),$$

where the final term, the fourth paradigm (ATR), indicates the macrotextual interactivity of author (A), text (T), and reader (R). In his seminal essay of 1971 'From Work to Text' (1977: 155–64), Roland Barthes famously distinguished between the 'readerly' or closed *work* (which can only be passively read) and the 'writerly' or entirely open *text* (which invites us to rewrite it as we read). We may thus rewrite our formula as

$$A \rightarrow work \rightarrow R \rightarrow text.$$

Even when the New Critics of our second paradigm, for example, talk about the 'text in itself,' they are clearly thinking of the 'text' as a closed product (rather than an open process), as a *work*, something 'wrought,' a completed, polished artefact.[6] We can thus add two further formulations:

A → text as product → R → text as process; and
A → text as work → R → text as play.

There is a patent and suggestive correspondence between this historical shift in the self-understanding of reading (functioning syntagmatically or 'horizontally') and the four levels of narrative (functioning paradigmatically or 'vertically') analysed here: from story to text to narration to textuality. Readers of the first paradigm placed overriding emphasis on what 'really' happened in the world of the story presented; second-paradigm readers like the New Critics consciously limited themselves rather to the 'text in itself,' 'the words upon the page'; the reader theory of the third paradigm emphasized the role of the literary text as semiotic communication, as bidirectional narration; while the post-structuralist textology of the fourth paradigm shifts the emphasis to the ludic textuality of the literary text, as reading becomes a potentially infinite three-way game of tag between reader, author, and text, infinitely deferring any decision as to who is 'it.' In the remainder of this chapter we shall discuss the play of textuality with specific reference to literary narrative, looking first at some textual games authors and readers play of their own volition and turning then to some textual games over which author and reader have little or no control.

In an obvious sense, every literary text is a game played by an author, who either invents a story or takes a ready-made story and in either event presents it in a form that, far from being a mere neutral, value-free, transparent container for that story, is carefully designed, whatever form that design may take, to exploit its own literary potential to the maximum. Within this overall game there are multiple subgames that authors can choose to play, and such games are that aspect of textual ludicity most frequently noted by the traditional reader, who will duly note and admire the author's irony, humour, wit, or what have you. A handy catalogue of such authorial games can be found in Peter Hutchinson's *Games Authors Play* (1983), and they need not be gone into any further here.

It is indicative for our present purposes, however, that Hutchinson completely ignores one particularly powerful game authors play, so powerful as to be almost invisible, namely the game involving the selection of *titles*. Titles may be referentially descriptive, with the primary emphasis variously on theme (*War and Peace*), character (*Madame Bovary*), setting (*Wuthering Heights*), or action (*Murder in the Cathedral*); they may be self-referentially descriptive (*A Portrait of the Artist as a Young Man*), intertextually allusive (*Ulysses, Finnegans Wake*), overtly symbolic (*The Trial, Heart of Darkness*), or ostensibly non-significant (*If on a Winter's Night a Traveler*); or they may be any one of multiple possible combinations and shadings of such alternatives. Whatever the title, the overall point is clear: before he has even had a chance to open the book he intends to read, the reader is already faced with a powerful opening move on the part of the author, one that will inevitably influence his own interpretive moves deeply. The reader of a text called *Madame Bovary* is directed from the moment he or she first encounters that particular title towards a very particular interpretive objective, namely the fullest possible understanding of what exactly is supposed to be so interesting about this particular character. If the text were called *Monsieur Bovary* or *Monsieur Homais* instead, the reader, even if no other word in the entire text were changed, would read it in a significantly different fashion.

One of the ground rules of literary narrative, in fact, is that the author is always in a position to cheat the reader if he or she chooses to do so, a position exploited in much post-modernist fiction: the reader's expectations are thus playfully thwarted, for example, in Flann O'Brien's *At Swim-Two-Birds*, which not only has three suggested different openings, but (like John Fowles's *The French Lieutenant's Woman*) three different conclusions as well.

Alain Robbe-Grillet's *La Maison de Rendez-vous* may similarly be seen as typical of texts that ostensibly encourage realist expectations while parodically refusing to adhere to them: a sofa is variously described by the narrator as 'yellow' (15), 'red ... or rather yellow' (20), 'red' (27, 39), 'yellow' (40), 'red-and-yellow striped' (40), and finally, as if tired of this relentless metamorphosis, 'colorless' (132); while the apartment of one of the characters is situated by the same narrator on the second (45), the fifth (81), the third or the fifth (87), and finally the seventh (150) floor of the building (O'Neill 1990: 264).

Authors, however, may play games, but they can never play them out, if only because of the games readers also (have to) play. The reader of the traditional paradigm whose role was to function solely as an empty vessel to be poured full with authorial meaning yields in the post-structuralist paradigm to a reader whose role is to cooperate with the author as co-producer, co-writer of a text whose final meaning resides not in a once-and-for-all interpretive product obtained by definitively crossing some hermeneutic finishing line but rather in a continuing, ludic process of interactive structuration. The post-structuralist text becomes a field of play on which author and reader play not what Bernard Suits has very usefully called a closed game, resulting in defeat for one contestant (as in such teleologically oriented games as football or tennis), but rather an open game, resulting in victory for both contestants simultaneously (as in games of make-believe, for example, where the object of the game is not to finish it but to keep it going) (Suits 1978: 131).

As readers, we are always also translators, always involved in metatextual activity, simultaneously free to exercise our own personality and our own best powers of interpretation on the one hand and constrained on the other both by what we find before us on the page and by what our cultural baggage *allows* us to find there. That cultural baggage both shapes us as readers, however, and simultaneously allows us to shape the text we read, for our decision, however involuntary, to read a particular text in a particular way is our greatest tool in shaping that text. The fact that an individual reader or community of readers chooses (or is led) to regard a text *as* a narrative, *as* fiction, *as* literary is, after all, a primary constituent factor of the text's textuality. Any ballad, say, to take just one example, changes very significantly when we decide to read it as primarily narrative rather than primarily poetic, fictional rather than non-fictional, or literary rather than non-literary.

The textualizing function of the reader, as previously mentioned, has been a matter of major concern for a number of years now for several different varieties of literary critic.[7] Approaches based on the premises of linguistic speech act theory have been particularly enlightening in drawing attention to the constitutive role of the reader in determining the 'literariness' or otherwise of given texts and thus effectively becoming their active co-producer rather than remaining simply the passive recipient of a finished product. Speech act theorists reject the formalist position that literature is formally and functionally distinct in its usage of language as opposed to the 'ordinary language' of everyday dealings. In other words, 'it is people, not properties, that "make a verbal message a verbal work of art" – people writing, editing, revising, reading, and judging. The specialness is in the context' (Pratt 1977: 124), and the context is their central characteristic of being known literary 'display texts' (143), which establishes the relevant 'appropriateness conditions' (Pratt 83). In other words, once we *know* (or believe we know) that a text is a literary text, we feel free to *read* it as a literary text – indeed we *make* it behave like a literary text. This shaping power of the reader is none the less strictly circumscribed: individual readers may conceivably choose (or be led) to regard a given text as literary in cases where such a response is not shared by others, but until their individual responses lose their idiosyncratic nature by being adopted by a larger interpretive community, such responses will be regarded as being to a greater or lesser degree aberrant, and the offender will be regarded as lacking in good taste or good sense or both.

The hedonistic game-playing author and reader of post-structuralist literary theory are not just players of their textual game, however, they are also themselves played by the games they play, and thus all reading, like all writing, comes to be seen as inevitably a palimpsest, a partly voluntary, partly involuntary structure of layerings. The author and the reader occupy the same relationship to the intertextual space in which they are situated as do actors to events on the level of story, partly shapers, partly shaped. Among the multiple and multiply interlinked currents constituting that space, the most potent in our current context of investigation is undoubtedly language itself, which, as Derridean grammatology and de Manian deconstruction have impressively demonstrated, through its uncontrollable etymologies, its variations of usage, its plays of meaning, its myriad conventions, is always a text in the poststructuralist sense, characterized by what Joyce, in another context, called an 'ineluctable modality,' where black can literally change to white before our very eyes. Durant and Fabb strikingly observe (1990: 18) that the etymological root of the word *black* is Indo-European **bhelg-* – which, however, meant something like 'white,' eventually giving us the Russian *belo-* 'white' as well as English *bleach* 'to make white' and *bald* 'having a white shining head.' Germanic *blakaz*, also derived from **bhelg-*, originally meant 'to have blazed brightly' – and, as of wood, turned *black* as a result. Far from being an exotic exception, moreover, post-structuralist language theorists would say, this is entirely typical of the way language functions as a system, permeated by a systemic ambiguity, a systemic capacity for prevarication (Lyons 1977: 83). Even where there is no intentional prevarication, it is clear that the particular context of utterance can radically influence the sense of an utterance. The set of implications accepted by one speaker as following from a given utterance may differ radically from the set accepted by another speaker as resulting from the same utterance (Lyons 1977: 205). Many perfectly acceptable utterances are inherently ambiguous, to the point where, for example, the sentence 'They passed the port at midnight' is subject to totally different interpretations according to whether 'port' is taken to refer to a harbour or to a fortified wine (Lyons 397). Further ambiguities may be introduced by what the semioticians would call channel noise, or by deficiencies in the language-users' competence or performance, as well as by the particular contexts in which the utterances occur – consider our party of maritime revellers enjoying an after-dinner drink as they slip past the nocturnal harbour, for example.

Umberto Eco argues, from a semiotic point of view, that 'usually a single sign-vehicle conveys many intertwined contents and therefore what is commonly called a "message" is in fact a *text* whose content is a multilevelled *discourse*' (1979: 57) – post-structuralist criticism sees literary texts as most centrally an institutionalization of this inherent instability of language. Eco sees the 'sememe' (or minimal unit of semantic content) as functioning less like a dictionary, with relatively rigid definitions of exact and unchanging meanings, than as an encyclopaedia, its meaning constituted by a network or 'compositional tree' of relationships frequently if not always of mutually opposed denotative and connotative features (1979: 84, 113). Like Barthes, Eco sees a central characteristic of aesthetic achievement in the 'programmed intertwining' (114) of the overlapping possible readings or paths constituting the spectrum of meaning of the individual linguistic sign-vehicles. The artistic achievement is thus centrally an intensification of forces already at work in all linguistic utterance, namely the complexity and unpredictability of sign production springing from the format of the semantic universe (142). Far from being merely a transparent medium for the undistorted transmission of information, language is grounded in paradox, in logical contradiction, and is thus, as the semantic theorist John Lyons argues, ultimately counterinformative, uninformative, in the sense of having not too little, but rather too much content (1977: 48). In such a context, to quote Eco, 'One might well ask whether the communicative process is capable of subduing the circumstances in which it takes place' (1979: 150). Post-structuralist critics would certainly answer that question with a resounding 'no.'

THE PLAY OF SUBVERSION

Narrative communication, then, involves both intratextual communication (between character and character, narrator and narratee, implied author and implied reader) and extratextual communication (between the real author and the real reader). Except that, as post-structuralist textology makes clear, reality is itself merely a fiction, and for *extratextual* we must read *intertextual*, which in its turn emerges as only another way of saying *intratextual*. The metatextual shapers are the intertextually shaped, all is text, and, in Derrida's famous formulation, 'there is nothing outside of the text' (1976: 158).

For reader theory before post-structuralism the reader seemed to be well on the way at last, happily and unproblematically, to usurping the position of textual authority previously occupied by the author. Wolfgang Iser thus sees the reading process as analogous to two people looking up at the night sky: the stars are the same, he says, but one observer will see a plough where the other will see a big dipper (1974: 282) – and we can extend the metaphor, for a third would see a bear, a fourth a carriage with horses, and a fifth only random twinklings of light. The author is allowed to fix the stars in their places, but the reader says what they mean. The productively playful reader suggested by a Barthes or a Derrida, on the other hand, is both infinitely freer and infinitely more constrained than Iser's reader, for unlike the fixed stars of Iser's model, the stars in the post-structuralist sky are never the 'same,' never identical with themselves, but always point instead to a meaning which is never quite there. The beguiling oedipal vision of the displaced author is only a vision after all, for even if the locus of authority has been displaced both from the author *and* from the words upon the page, it does not on that account take up immediate and untroubled residence with the reader either. The post-structuralist reader, however comparatively free he or she may be, can never be totally free.

The reader's response, however idiosyncratic, cannot be entirely *cause*, for it is (however provisionally) also part of the *effect* of the text. The receiver not only makes the text work, he is also made to make it work; but he can only be made to make it work if he chooses to make it work. This paradoxical, catch-22 interrelationship of freedom and determination, implicit in the semiotic account of the text as a communicational act, has become a major focus of deconstructionist thought. The process of 'reading' a text, once conceived of as purely a practical matter of sticking in a thumb and pulling out a plum, deconstructs theoretically into a logical impossibility, a self-sustaining paradox. The thrust of post-structuralist thinking, in short, has been not wholly to eliminate authority, but to relocate it, and its new locus is precisely in tex-tuality itself – and thus in paradox, the aporia and absent centre around which all deconstructionist thinking endlessly circles. 'What happens in literary semiotics is but one version of a general situ-ation which is gradually coming to be recognized as an inescap-able feature of our ways of thinking about texts and significa-tion,' as Jonathan Culler writes (1981: 39), namely the revelation of paradox as an inherent component of our concept of meaning.

Finally, we may return to the question whether a consideration of textuality has any valid place in the theoretical study of narra-tive specifically as narrative. Classical narratology in the French tradition answers this question in the negative and retains a strictly intratextual range of operation, as we have seen – but even within its chosen boundaries classical narratology is far from being a monolith, and there are, as we have seen, already quite funda-mental differences among its adherents, most notably as to whether two narrative levels (story and discourse) or three (story, text, narration) should be seen as minimally necessary for the proper analysis of narrative and, even more crucially, as to what the most appropriate number of narrative agents should be seen as being. Thus Bal and Rimmon-Kenan, as we may remember, strongly emphasize the role of the narrator and the narratee, but disqualify the implied author and the implied reader from their consideration of the narrative transaction altogether; Chatman gives the implied author and the implied reader pride of place in his version of the cast, but sees the narrator and narratee as merely optional; more recently, Toolan sees the real author, the narrator, and the real reader as the only essential participants in the narra-tive transaction, with the narratee as merely an optional fourth (1988: 77). There is, in short, no compelling reason for viewing narratology as a closed rather than an open game.

To repeat an observation made earlier: the whole concept of narrative structure is in a sense no more than a convenient fiction, and there is no particular reason why different investigators should end up with fictions that are identical. The point, once again, is the degree to which the fictions involved are productively useful ones, for particular purposes in particular contexts of investigation. In our consideration of the subversive element in narrative discourse it is abundantly clear that without appropriate analysis of the role of textuality our story would remain radically incomplete. Indeed, the paradoxical process of discursive subversion that emerges in our particular context of investigation as central to narrative communication is clearly not only continued but raised to a higher power on the level of textuality, for if story is subverted by discourse on the intratextual level, as argued in earlier chapters, it is very evident that on the extratextual level, as we may provisionally (and duplicitously) continue to call (or narrate) it, discourse subverts itself.

6

Games Texts Play:
Reading between the Narratives

One particularly interesting area where the story of the literary text is taken up and reshaped by readers who also function simultaneously and very overtly as writers is that of literary translation. In our final chapter we shall therefore begin by looking at some everyday (but none the less fascinating) questions concerning the implications of translation, continue by comparing three quite different theoretical models of translation, and conclude by sketching the beginnings of an intertextual experiment that by definition can never be completed.

QUESTIONS OF TRANSLATION

Roman Jakobson (1959) distinguishes three types of translation: *interlingual*, or translation 'proper,' namely between natural languages; *intralingual*, or interpretation by means of other verbal signs within the same language; and *intersemiotic*, or transposition into a different system of signs, such as a film version of a written narrative.[1] Intersemiotic translation in particular poses some especially interesting questions with regard to the whole concept of translation and its implications.

One of the quite extraordinary – though very largely unnoticed – conventions of film, for example, is the treatment of 'foreign' languages. Luchino Visconti's film *Death in Venice* (1971) is a double translation of Thomas Mann's story *Der Tod in Venedig* (1912), in that it is, first, an intersemiotic translation from literary to filmic discourse and, second, an interlingual translation (with very considerable freedoms) from Mann's German to the film's English. In the opening scenes, the German protagonist Gustav von Aschenbach, en route to Venice by boat, spends his time reading German books and German newspapers, as the camera clearly shows us, but when he speaks what we invariably hear is English. We are, of course, not at all surprised by this, for since the film was made in English for English-speaking audiences we fully expect to be able to understand what Aschenbach (played by the British actor Dirk Bogarde) is saying. But what language is Aschenbach 'really' speaking? When he addresses the Venetian gondolier who delivers him to his hotel or the Italian-speaking hotel manager, for example, what we hear is English, but are we to assume that this is 'really' German, understood and spoken flawlessly by the two Italians? The point is not that we never hear any language other than English, for when the gondolier mutters to himself or when the hotel manager addresses the desk clerk or the porters the actors playing them speak Italian, just as the actors playing the Polish boy Tadzio and his friends speak Polish (and occasionally French) to each other. This might suggest a convention that Bogarde's English is indeed 'really' Aschenbach's German. But when Aschenbach (in a flashback) is speaking to his German composer friend – Bogarde's English presumably still corresponding to Aschenbach's German – and the German housemaid Rosa enters and announces that 'Der Tee ist serviert,' Aschenbach duly thanks her, but *still* in Bogarde's English. Now, if Rosa is 'really' speaking German – as the actor playing her certainly is – what language is Aschenbach *now* 'really' speaking? Obviously German still, we assume. The unspoken implication here, and in a multitude of similar cases, is evidently that the actor playing Rosa can *afford* to speak German either because what she says is readily comprehensible ('Guten Tag,' 'Bonjour,' 'Prego') or because it doesn't *matter* whether we understand what she says or not. On the one hand, that is to say, there is the (story-oriented) element of 'local colour' necessary to serve the needs of an apparently realistic portrayal; on the other there is the (discourse-oriented) criterion of narrative relevance.

If the criterion of realistic portrayal were the sole criterion, then all characters would have to speak only those languages in which they were ('really') competent. If discursive relevance were the only criterion, on the other hand, then all of the 'foreigners' – and Aschenbach, whom we hear speaking English, is evidently not to be regarded as a foreigner in this sense – could in fact speak the *same* language (or a total gibberish, for that matter) as long as the result was simply incomprehensible noise.

A slightly different variation on this theme occurs when we hear screen Nazis in old Hollywood movies talking among themselves in heavily German-accented American English where the foreign-accented English punctuated by occasional German expressions like *Achtung!* or *Dummkopf!* conventionally indicates that these are *foreigners* – from the English-speaking point of view – speaking a presumably *accent-free* native German. A similar problem in literary texts is that of translating non-standard language usage. Should a character who speaks with a strong Bavarian accent, for example, be translated into standard English or transposed into Irish brogue, Scots burr, or Tennessee drawl? Clearly, different receptive contexts will dictate different decisions on the part of different translators, and none of these decisions will ever be entirely satisfactory.

Hamlet's speaking only in blank verse also presents problems of a somewhat similar nature (although with a greater emphasis on the relationship of figure and ground) in terms of what he is 'really' doing: if the actor's verse equals Hamlet's 'ordinary language,' for example, how would the actor have to behave if Hamlet chose to recite a poem? Opera, ballet, and stage or screen musicals present us with the same conundrum. Are the characters 'really' dancing *pas de deux* or, like Mimi in *La Bohème*, 'really' singing lustily for ten minutes, propped on one elbow, before expiring of tuberculosis? Why does the villainous Pizarro in Beethoven's *Fidelio*, surprised by Fidelio/Leonora in his attempt to murder the unjustly imprisoned Florestan, and with a trumpet call urgently warning him that justice is about to catch up with him, pause long enough to engage in a very beautiful quartet with Florestan, Fidelio, and the jailer before belatedly attempting to flee? The answer, of course, is that he does nothing of the sort; as far as the story-world is concerned the quartet never takes place, it exists only on the level of discourse; it is not part of the action, it is part of a particular mode of presentation.

So how can we best describe the narrative structure here? Does the character Pizarro live in a possible world where time stands still while its inhabitants periodically burst into song, for example? Does the Hamlet who kills Polonius, as opposed to the actor who plays Hamlet, need to have an ear for blank verse? Does the Pizarro who imprisons Florestan need to be able to sing? He hears the trumpet, but can he hear the violins? Evidently, in fact, we could say that Pizarro hears the trumpet because there is a trumpet in the orchestral 'discourse' playing the *role* of a trumpet in the story. Operas, musicals, and verse dramas alike, indeed, employ narrative conventions that, as vehicles of narrative, may well strike us initially as ludicrously inefficient. But these conventions are different from 'standard' (literary) narrative techniques only in degree rather than in kind: there is no essential difference between Pizarro's aria suspending story-time and a literary narrator who (à la Tristram Shandy) puts his narrative temporarily on hold while indulging in essayistic speculations that may take several pages or even chapters to complete before returning to his suspended hero. While some of the implications of translation (once we notice them in the first place) may thus initially strike us as distinctly exotic, in the end translation, whether interlingual, intralingual, or intersemiotic, is in all important ways simply another name for reading – which in very important ways is another name for writing.

MODELS OF TRANSLATION

'Someone must have traduced Joseph K., for without having done anything wrong he was arrested one fine morning,' Willa and Edwin Muir felicitously open their 1937 translation of Franz Kafka's unfinished novel *The Trial*, though in later editions the expression 'traduced' is replaced by the more pedestrian 'been telling lies about' (1). In the present chapter we shall be concerned with the traducing not of Joseph K. but of Franz Kafka – with the translation of Kafka, that is to say, for while one now obsolete meaning of the verb 'to traduce' is indeed 'to translate,' its only current meaning is precisely 'to tell lies about,' and in one sense translation is always a calculated process of telling lies about its object of interest. Kafka, after all, clearly wanted his text to read neither 'Someone must have traduced Joseph K.' nor 'Someone must have been telling lies about Joseph K.' but rather 'Jemand musste Josef K. verleumdet haben' (*Der Prozess* 7). What is perhaps not so clear is who (or what) this 'Kafka' I can talk about so glibly here was (or is). For most of us, most of the time, certainly, it is merely a commonplace and completely untroubling metonymy to say that we are reading 'Kafka' or 'Dostoevsky' or 'Molière' when what we are really reading is the body of work produced by them. Nor, usually, is the metonymy any more troubling if the texts we are actually reading happen to be in translation rather than the original, and few of us would consider we were being anything less than totally truthful in claiming to have read, say, the Bible, even if we were completely ignorant of either Hebrew or Greek. Likewise, as avid readers, we have all certainly read Homer and Virgil, Dante and Goethe, Cervantes and Shakespeare, Tolstoy and Proust. Or have we? Are we really being as entirely accurate as we may think we are?

The notion that translation is always more or less a tissue of lies on a more obvious level is, of course, an easy commonplace, a popular wisdom. 'Traduttore, traditore,' as the Italian aphorism has it, 'Translator, traitor.' These traitors' translations in turn, as the matching French aphorism, with cheerful sexism, puts it, are like 'les belles infidèles' – the more beautiful they are, the less likely they are to be faithful.[2] And the contemporary analogue of this wisdom is that the movie, as we all know, is never as good as the book. Exceptions merely prove the general, if more or less unquestioned rule. But what does 'as good as' mean? What constitutes treason? How do we measure fidelity? What, in other words, are the concepts of textual *authority* that underwrite, *inter alia*, our notions of evaluation as far as translation is concerned?

Traditionally, translation has been imbued with and surrounded by what one might call a quasi-religious myth of originality. We see this at work, for example, in a statement such as Horst Frenz's that 'in general, translations date more quickly than their original' (1973: 119). Why, we might well ask ourselves, should this be so? Pope's translation of Homer, for example, began to appear in 1715, just a year after the appearance of one of his 'own' works, *The Rape of the Lock*. Have these two texts really aged over the intervening centuries at differential rates? And if so, why? And what does 'in general' mean? Perhaps it refers to that other common manifestation of the myth of originality, the casual and widespread assumption that translations by 'real authors already' are somehow superior, better, more the 'real thing' than translations by individuals who are *not* real authors but merely members of that presumably inferior literary breed, translators, who by definition are incapable of producing the real thing – unless, of course, like Pope, they write a book of their 'own,' an *original* text, which then, by definition, will at least have some defensible claim to being considered the 'real thing.' And again, what of 'translations' that turn out not to have been translations after all? James Macpherson's alleged translations in the 1760s from the Gaelic of Ossian, for example, eventually turned out to be simple forgeries. But simple forgeries in this case meant Macpherson's own original work. Does he (or should he), any moral or legal considerations aside, consequently occupy a rightfully higher rank in literary history precisely *because* he was a literary swindler? Where, in other words, is the 'real thing' here? Is there, indeed, any such thing, here or elsewhere, as the real thing?

The myth of originality reveals itself most obviously in the master/servant relationship that has traditionally obtained between so-called original texts and their translations – or, more accurately, between original authors and their translators. In this relationship the translator's task was to become as transparent, as inconspicuous, in a word, as *absent* as possible in order that the creative originality of the author might shine through unimpeded and unimpaired. This model of translation, moreover, was only one aspect of a larger model of reading in general, for even the original author's work was itself to some degree already a translation, since literary works are constructed out of language, and the task of language in this relationship was likewise to become as transparent and inconspicuous and essentially absent as possible in order that the real *meaning* of the author might shine through without distortion or distraction. The formula governing the relationship of original and translation was thus as follows: the original author is to the transparent translator as original meaning is to transparent language. Or as master is to servant, for in this scheme of things translation serves 'literature,' which in turn serves truth.[3]

So whom are you reading when you read Kafka in translation? Under the traditional dispensation, as outlined here, the answer could only be that one read *as if* reading Kafka: on the one hand what one read *was* really Kafka, but on the other hand it was not *really* Kafka, but Kafka through a glass – a more or less dirty glass – darkly. The translator, essentially an impostor, was essentially also more or less of a nuisance – and ideally less, of course, for the ideal translator in this scheme of things is entirely invisible, writes himself (like the Cheshire Cat) entirely out of existence, out of the text. There is one author, and the disappearing translator is his maximally self-effacing prophet.

Thus the traditional model of translation, based on the twin pillars of authorial originality and authorial authority – and deriving ultimately from the essentially religious concept, at once theocentric and theocratic, of a divine revelation. In the aftermath of structuralism and its assorted developments, however, there has been a paradigm shift in the late-twentieth-century concept of the role of the translator, just as there has been in the case of the literary critic. The new paradigm is based less on the mysteries of divine revelation than on the semiotics of literary communication and owes less to the radically centralized power structure of pre-industrial political and religious autocracy than to the decentralized structures of information management in our (post-)modern, (post-)democratic, (post-)industrial Western societies.

My aim here is not to attempt any would-be comprehensive outline of contemporary translation theories.[4] It can none the less be confidently asserted that one of their crucial common factors is the notion of textuality, more specifically the notion that all translations are first and foremost *metatexts* – that is to say, linguistic texts *about* other linguistic texts. This metatextual model of translation practice sees all translation as essentially compound discourse, discourse about other discourse, and as a result the authority that was formerly seen as residing solely and unshakeably with the historical, empirical author and his inalienable claim to originality is now seen as displaceable throughout an entire textual system, which includes not only the author and *his* text but also a potentially infinite series of translators, who may subsequently, as new 'authors,' create their 'own' texts based to a greater or lesser degree on their encounter with this one, originary text. Each of the new 'Kafkas' produced under this new theoretical dispensation has a more or less defensible claim to being the 'real' Kafka, for that reality is now grounded in textual rather than biographical authority, whether or not the text under analysis is the only true original or a displaced variant of it.

Again, this new model of translation is also only one aspect of a more general model of reading – whose broader resonances may also be observed in areas of critical practice not owing any direct allegiance to structuralist ideas in the narrower sense, such as the New Critical theory of the autotelic text. In the metatextual model of compound discourse author A produces text B, which is read by reader C. But readers are of very different kinds, and their processing of the textual information is infinitely variable. Indeed, in this scheme of things no reader *can* ever read the same text twice, for as individuals we are subject throughout our existence to ineluctable change, and the texts we read change with us. Some readers, moreover, are more productive than other readers, and while every reader potentially produces his or her own text in processing the text of author A, some readers go on to actually write down their own texts, in which case one of the labels we can give to such readers is that of translator. Every translator is both a reader and an author, in other words, and every translator of Kafka, for example, constructs in the required target language, as author, an analogue to the Kafka he or she has reconstructed as a reader in the source language of the text. But this is essentially true of any reader, for all our readings are always simultaneously reconstructions and re-constructions, decodings and encodings, taking apart and putting together again a text that is simultaneously the same and uniquely different. A translator, in short, under the new theoretical dispensation, is nothing more or less than a fully consistent reader, a reader with the courage of his or her convictions. Every translation of Kafka is a new reading of Kafka, and every reading is at least potentially a new translation.

So, once again, who (and where) is Kafka? For the traditional model of the older paradigm, as we have seen, Kafka is a unique historical individual of genius, born in Prague in 1883, the unique locus of the text's authority (whether in translation or not), the ultimate origin of all its meaning – and essentially the same for every reader. For the metatextual model of the new paradigm, on the other hand, authority is displaced from the original author to the interaction of individual texts and individual readers, and 'Kafka' is the Kafka constructed by each individual reader in a proliferating string of readings (whether in translation or not). But it is also possible, still operating by the game rules of the new paradigm, to theorize a third – if entirely 'impractical' – answer to the question, which we may call the intertextual model. For this model, Kafka is neither a unique and unchanging individual nor a proliferation of endlessly variable individual readings but rather an entire shifting *system* of potentially endless variable readings, the *sum*, that is to say, of all the translations and readings of Kafka that have ever existed or will ever exist in any language. If the locus of textual authority was firmly identified with the historical, empirical author in our first model (which is pre-structuralist in its assumptions), and displaced on to individual textual encounters in the second (essentially structuralist in its assumptions), in the third, which is post-structuralist in its assumptions, the locus of authority is dispersed, disseminated, diffused throughout the entire textual system.

This translation of authority is, once again, by no means limited to translated texts, for all three of these models are models of reading *tout court* rather than just of reading translations. Texts in translation, however, provide a particularly graphic set of examples of the issues involved. Authority is essentially extratextual in the first model, the traditional reader reading *through* the words on the page (whether translated or not) to the living thoughts and intentions of the unique and uniquely authoritative historical author. In the second model authority is essentially metatextual in that it begins with the concrete text on the page, sometimes actually and always potentially translated by the further textualizing process of its reception by successive readers. In the third model authority is essentially intertextual, for this model, subscribing to post-structuralist conceptions of textuality, duly holds that a Kafka read in Spanish cannot be the 'same' Kafka read in French or English or German, that your Kafka is not my Kafka, and that my Kafka today is not my Kafka of yesterday or tomorrow – and yet all of these synecdochic Kafkas together comprise the macrotext we also call 'Kafka,' the Kafka phenomenon, the Kafka system. Where the traditional model is unitary (one Kafka for all readings), and the metatextual model is pluralist (one Kafka for each reading), the intertextual model is theoretically holistic (since all possible readings *constitute* one Kafka). The ultimate sum of this intertextual system, of course, must always remain incalculable, and its 'one' Kafka ungraspable, not merely because of the linguistic and other limitations of individual readers, but because any attempt to sum the system would inevitably be an exercise in paradox, since the macro-Kafka it produced would then have to be included in a new mapping, and so on in an endless circular regress.

MAPPING THE UNMAPPABLE

The impossibility of the endeavour as a whole need not deter us from exploring the beginnings of one or two of its proliferating pathways, however, and we shall now turn our attention to this experiment. To this purpose the reader will find an appendix at the end of this chapter containing the opening and closing sentences of Kafka's narrative *Das Urteil* (1913) – in the original German, three different English translations, two French versions, two Italian versions, and one Spanish rendering. Ideally the selection should, of course, be very much larger, but it will suffice to demonstrate the general principle of the intertextual model.

The story of *Das Urteil* ('The Judgment'), to establish the context, is quickly summarized: Georg Bendemann, a young businessman, writes to a bachelor friend in Russia to announce his recent engagement and shortly thereafter informs his elderly father that he has just written the letter. Whereupon his father accuses him (a) of having invented the friend and (b) of having disgraced his dead mother's memory by the planned marriage. Moreover, (c) the friend, non-existent or not, is really *his* friend; (d) the girl would be his too, if he wished; and (e) since Georg had always wished his father dead, now *he* sentences Georg himself to death, by drowning. Georg rushes from the house and throws himself off a bridge.[5] Let us now proceed to look at some selected phrases in all nine of the versions before us – but with the specific understanding that we are *not* going to treat one as the original and the other eight as more or less unsuccessful renderings, but rather (and this is the point of our experiment) that we shall treat all nine as a single multivoiced, translingual 'original,' an interweaving and interwovenness of voices in which the individual voices will sometimes agree and sometimes differ – but each voice will always relativize each of the others and, in so doing, put itself continually in question as well. We can, to begin with, let Kafka's German be our point of departure, a privileged voice, but this is a matter merely of convenience rather than necessity, since we could just as easily declare one or other of the French or the Spanish versions to be our privileged voice and the German version to be just one more of the many other competing voices. Ideally, no single one of the individual voices would be privileged for the purposes of this exercise, the multipart (and metaphorical) harmony of these textual spheres emerging precisely from the interplay of all the voices simultaneously, with now one and now another of them seizing our attention by virtue of a particularly brilliantly or strikingly executed effect.[6] (In order to suggest something of the nature of this interplay I shall refer to the versions only by the letter and number identifying them in the appendix, rather than by the name of their individual authors.)

'Es war an einem Sonntagvormittag im schönsten Frühjahr,' begins the German A1. We notice that while the German superlative 'im *schönsten* Frühjahr' ostensibly draws attention to the beauty of this time of year, only two of the other voices do so, the French A5 referring to 'la beauté du printemps' and the Italian A8 to the 'momento più bello della primavera.' The English voices all prefer to employ a metaphor of height instead – 'in the (very) height of spring' – a metaphor that will become startlingly concrete in the climactic scene of the narrative, when Georg's father springs to his feet on the bed, even touching the ceiling with one hand to steady himself, as he pronounces his fatal judgment from on high. The Spanish A9 employs a metaphor of fullness instead – 'en plena primavera' – while the French A6 ironically speaks of 'une année qui débutait splendidement,' echoed by the Italian A7, 'faceva un tempo splendido.' 'Georg,' as he is called in German and Spanish and by two of the English voices, metamorphoses into 'George' in A4, 'Georges' in both French voices, and 'Giorgio' for both Italian voices, a cultural change of key interestingly paralleling the polarity of familiarity and strangeness informing the relationship of Georg (as we may continue to call him) and his nameless friend in a stylized Russia. Georg is 'ein junger Kaufmann' in A1, a 'merchant' in A2, a 'businessman' in A3 and A4, a 'commerciante' in A7 and A8, a 'comerciante' in A9. For both of the French voices, however, he is 'un jeune négociant,' and this catches with absolute precision the element of competition and rivalry that will emerge as existing between Georg and his Russian friend on the one hand, Georg and his father on the other. A 'négociant' is one who negotiates, employs strategies, devises game plans, in order to gain a superior position, and the course of the struggle between Georg and his father that will come to dominate the story can be traced in detail as constituting a series of such antagonistic game situations. (If I might interrupt the rules of my own game momentarily and interject a comment of an evaluative nature at this point, by the way, here is surely one example of a translation that is clearly superior to the original – but only, of course, for the purposes of this particular interpretive angle.)

Georg's friend in Russia is described in German as being 'im Ausland,' which on the one hand simply means 'abroad,' as all three English versions neutrally phrase it, but also, and far less neutrally, 'l'étranger' of both French voices, the 'estero' of both Italian voices, and 'el extranjero' of the Spanish.[7] Georg 'hatte gerade einen Brief an [diesen] sich im Ausland befindenden Jugendfruend beendet [und] verschloss ihn in spielerischer Langsamkeit,' according to A1. We notice in passing the polarity of youth and age between the 'Jugendfreund' of the German and the 'old friend' of two of the English voices. We notice, too, that while for all the English and French and one of the Italian voices the friend was quite neutrally 'living' abroad – 'résidant' (A5), 'habitait' (A6), 'viveva' (A8) – in German he is 'sich im Ausland befindend,' and for the Spanish (echoed less forcefully in the Italian A7) the friend likewise 'se encontraba en el extranjero,' which taken completely literally means 'he met himself (or found himself) in that which was strange.'[8] Would Georg, too, 'find' himself, 'meet' himself as if he were a stranger, if he, too, had the courage or the resolve or whatever it took to risk leaving the security of the known and the familiar for the unknown and the strange?

There are (at least) two sides to everything, of course – including writing a letter, which for A1 Georg had just 'beendet.' For two of the English voices (A2, A3) he had just 'finished' this letter, just as for both Italian voices he 'aveva finito,' or in other words had simply ceased to write any more, while for the third English voice he had 'completed' it, or in other words had brought it to a successful conclusion. The same tension is exactly reflected in the two French voices: A6 prefers 'terminer,' simply to reach an end, while A5 prefers the more active 'achever,' to achieve or bring about an end, a choice also favoured by the Spanish, where Georg 'acababa de escribir,' which taken quite rigorously at its word – like the French 'achever' – means that he had brought his writing to a head. We notice, incidentally, that the Spanish is the only voice that actually mentions 'escribir' 'writing' at this point

– all the other voices, including the German, simply refer to the finishing or completion of 'a letter,' 'einen Brief,' 'une lettre,' 'una lettera,' 'una carta.'

This letter Georg had put in its envelope 'mit spielerischer Langsamkeit,' and the elusiveness of his possible motivation here is reflected in the variety of interpretations given to this phrase in the different voices: for A2 it was done in a 'slow and dreamy fashion,' for A3 he 'toyed with it,' for A4 it was done with 'frivolous deliberation,' for A6 it was simply 'avec lenteur' and for A7 'lentamente,' while A5 is clear that it was 'avec une lenteur feinte,' A8 talks of a 'lentezza compiaciuta, quasi giocherellando,' and A9 has it done 'distraída y lánguidamente.' The complexity of Georg's motivation here is a reflection of the complex processes that ostensibly impelled his alleged friend to leave home. This nameless friend had been 'mit seinem Fortkommen zu Hause unzufrieden,' as the German puts it in a deconstructive *double entendre*. 'Fortkommen' is progress, but it is also 'getting away,' and 'zu Hause,' staying at home, is the familiar stumbling-block to both. Two of the English voices (A3, A4) have him dissatisfied merely with his 'progress,' just as for A7 he is 'scontento della sua esistenza in famiglia,' and one of the French likewise (A6) has him 'mécontent de piétiner au pays,' dissatisfied with marking time, shuffling his feet. The other French voice (A5) has him 'insatisfait de la situation qu'on lui avait faite,' where progress has more overtly given way to stasis, and this is a situation that has ostensibly been thrust upon him, apparently through no fault or desire of his own. The passivity of his 'situation' and the unattainability of any active 'progress' leads in A2 to his being 'dissatisfied with his *prospects*' (emphasis added), as also in the Spanish A9, where he is 'disconforme con las perspectivas que su patria le ofrecía.' The 'prospects' and 'perspectivas' here are parodically reflected in the view or prospect observed by Georg from his window in the same paragraph, while the Spanish also not only alerts us through its use of 'perspectivas' to the various game strategies that will be employed in the narrative but also stresses both the passivity of the friend – who is 'offered' prospects – and the power to offer or withhold of the 'patria,' the land precisely of the father(s). The Italian A7 echoes the passivity but not the *nom du père* of the Spanish: the friend was 'insoddisfatto per quanto gli offriva il suo paese.'

This friend, Georg reflects in A1, '[hatte sich] vor Jahren schon nach Russland ... förmlich geflüchtet.' He 'had actually run away' according to A2, 'had quite simply decamped' according to A3, had 'quite literally escaped' according to A4. But 'literally' and 'förmlich' are both slippery words, and this is – once again – well caught by the difference between the two French voices, A6 with 'littéralement enfui,' A5 with 'pour ainsi dire enfui.' Everything that happens in a literary text is both 'literal' and 'so to speak,' 'pour ainsi dire.' It is precisely the moment of indecision between the actual and the possible here and throughout *Das Urteil* that gives the text its compellingly provocative and enigmatic character.

Das Urteil, in biographical terms, can clearly be read as being *about* necessary decisions that were vital for Kafka at this point in his life: the decision whether to leave home or not, whether to stand up to his father once and for all or not, whether to risk marriage or not, and no doubt most important of all, whether any of these other decisions would endanger the one decision he had already and irrevocably taken, namely to go on writing at all costs. But *Das Urteil* is a literary text, and therefore its aboutness is more important than what it is about, its allusiveness is more important than its referentiality, its status as a literary, self-reflexive text is more important – for us as literary critics at any rate – than its status as a real-world biographical text. Kafka, notoriously, confided to Max Brod that when he wrote the last sentence of *Das Urteil* – 'In diesem Augenblick ging über die Brücke ein geradezu unendlicher Verkehr' (which the reader will find below in voices B1 to B9) – he was thinking of a powerful sexual ejaculation, 'eine starke Ejakulation' (Neumann 1981: 36). The serious-minded Brod, perennial Boswell to Kafka's Johnson, duly went away and wrote this down for posterity, and we need not concern ourselves here with the exact degree to which his scholarly leg was being pulled. As readers of a literary text, however, *our* leg is always being pulled, for the literary text always, by its very nature, says one thing and means another.

The friend in Russia, 'wie er erzählte, hatte ... keine rechte Verbindung mit der dortigen Kolonie seiner Landsleute, aber auch fast keinen gesellschaftlichen Verkehr mit einheimischen Familien und richtete sich so für ein endgültiges Junggesellentum ein.' In this shadow world of 'Verkehr,' where 'Landsleute' are strangers and strangers are 'einheimisch,' the nameless friend has 'fast keinen ... Verkehr,' no 'intercourse,' as all three English voices have it, no 'relation sociale' for A5, no 'rapport' for A6, no 'rapporti' for A7 and A8, no 'amistades' for A9, a friend in name who is nobody's friend in deed. When the 'geradezu unendlicher Verkehr' passes over the bridge of the last paragraph, the same bridge we already know from the first paragraph but from which Georg has now let himself drop, there is (pace Max Brod) no 'intercourse' in the English versions anymore, only an 'unending,' 'endless' 'stream of traffic,' 'un trafic immense,' as the French B5 puts it, 'un traffico interminabile' for B7. As interpreters, critics, translators, *readers* in short, we are in a sense all part of that endless traffic over Kafka's bridge, 'una interminable fila,' as the Spanish has it, 'un interminabile andirivieni' for the Italian B8, interminably going and coming, filing past, circling around the Kafkan text, in what B6 calls 'une circulation littéralement folle.'

One final – or initial – key phrase with which to conclude our prelude to an endless reading of a tiny fragment of the Kafka system: the title. 'Das Urteil' is rendered by all three English voices as 'The Judg(e)ment' and by the French A5 likewise as 'Le jugement.' But judgment is only one aspect of the threefold process that constitutes a judicial 'Urteil,' which contains first the process of forming a judgment, then the judicial utterance of the verdict reached, and finally the imposition of the punishment appropriate to the crime. The English title 'The Judg(e)ment' and the French 'Le jugement' emphasize the first aspect of this process, the formation of a judicial opinion. The second aspect is emphasized by the second French title, 'Le verdict,' the speaking of what is now judicial truth (*verum dictare*), and the third is underlined both by the Italian 'La condanna' and by the Spanish 'La condena,' the condemnation, the imposition of the sentence. The final step in the judicial process exceeds the reach of the title in any of the languages examined here, namely the execution of the sentence, the death by drowning imposed by Georg's father. But, we might well ask ourselves, is that sentence in fact ever carried out? We see Georg, his own apparent executioner, let himself drop from the bridge, indeed. What we do not see is Georg ever reaching the water, much less drowning. Suspended between the inception and the completion of the act of self-execution, Georg finally leaves the readers of *Das Urteil* where they have always been, faced with the necessity of forming their own judgment, passing their own sentence, executing their own decision.

AFTER ARCHIMEDES

For our first model of reading, the traditional, pre-structuralist model, translation is essentially a reluctantly tolerated but sometimes necessary evil allowing readers to approach the work of authors otherwise linguistically inaccessible. The grateful reader's reaction is to ignore the translation as much as possible, indeed to treat it as non-existent after due reassurance by competent authorities that it is as faithful as possible to the original work he or she would preferably be reading directly rather than at one remove. For the second, the metatextual model of reading, drawing on structuralist concepts of textual interaction, translation emerges, in a dramatic paradigm shift, from this state of marginalized toleration to become the very template of all reading, all interpretation. For the first model, founded on the centrality of original, authorial authority, the reader reads *in spite of* a translation; for the second model, decentred, destabilized, and founded on the fragmentation of authority, translation is the only option there can ever be. For the third, the intertextual model of reading, drawing on post-structuralist notions of textual interaction, all the possible 'translations' together *constitute* a parodic new, but endlessly inaccessible 'original' – authority recentred (if only through the looking-glass), but centre and circle coincide, and their circumference is incalculable.

Intriguing though the concept might be in theoretical terms, our intertextual, macrotextual model might also seem at first sight to be little more than a self-sufficient and self-indulgent academic game, a donnish joke, of the kind in which contemporary literary theory increasingly abounds. And, indeed, if taken exclusively as a model of translation, our third model obviously has extremely limited practical possibilities, since very few readers will be able to go in any meaningful way beyond a comparative consideration of translations in three or four of the more familiar foreign languages. Once again, however, the macrotextual model of translation is only one aspect of a more general model of reading, and for all that its paradoxical nature is abundantly clear once we attempt to employ it comprehensively, we all, in fact, use it quite practically and quite regularly – indeed potentially always – in our reading of literary texts, even if we may do so both largely unconsciously and in a very much reduced application. 'My' *Odyssey*, for example, is made up not of a single text immaculately preserved in my mind, but rather is the result of several different readings, at several different ages, in several different places, with several different degrees of concentration, background, knowledge, and insight, of several different translations, combined with occasional study over two or three decades of selected passages in the original Greek, more or less eroded memories of lectures I have heard and books and articles I have read over many years on Homer, not to mention various half-understood popular treatments of the tale or parts of it read or seen since childhood in comic books, abbreviated and simplified children's versions, the movies, and on TV.[9] What is true of my *Odyssey* is equally true of my Homer, my Dante, my Shakespeare, my Kafka – and my 'Kafka' is not your 'Kafka,' nor yours mine.

Most of the time, of course, when I sit down as a critic to examine a literary text, I merely allow this macrotextual, intertextual, contextual information to function, more or less unconsciously, as a background of general knowledge to my more immediate endeavours. On a more conscious level, I essentially have to decide whether to operate according to the rules of either our first model or our second model, and if I should happen to be dealing with matters involving translation this will eventually bring me back, sooner or later, to the question of evaluation. As long as I adhere to the traditional model of reading, neither the traditional questions nor the traditional answers have changed, and fidelity to (assumed) authorial intention remains the unshakeable touchstone. Once I choose to operate by the rules of the second model, however, I am immediately faced with the question as to how one is supposed to evaluate a translation in this brave but unstable new world of floating authority.

The most productive answer here seems clearly to be that any evaluation will be based less usefully on traditional notions of fidelity to authorial norms than it will be on the same criteria we can most usefully employ when judging the relative validity of *any* of competing sets of readings or interpretations. These are spelled out in exemplary fashion by Paul Armstrong (1983: 346–7), and they are three in number. The first of them is the criterion of inclusiveness: any interpretation – and every translation is an interpretation – should capture a maximum of the information present in the text interpreted. To translate the title 'Das Urteil' by 'The Decision,' for example, or 'The Sentence,' both of which options could be argued for to a certain point, would clearly fail to meet the criterion of inclusiveness, since neither captures nuances of meaning that, as we have seen, can be regarded as crucial to the narrative. The second criterion is that of persuasiveness: to translate the title as 'The Opinion,' for example, would not only fail to be inclusive but would also signally fail to exercise any power of persuasion that this was indeed the most appropriate solution. The third criterion is that of suggestiveness, and here the translation of the word 'Kaufmann' by the French 'négociant' rather than the English 'merchant' or 'businessman,' as discussed above, provides an excellent example of how this criterion is brilliantly met in this instance by the French and met with only marginal adequacy by the English.

These are minimal cases, of course, dealing with single words or phrases only. The problem becomes massively more complicated when we attempt to evaluate a five-hundred-page or a thousand-page translation. But this is as it has always been, and there is no getting away from it: every translation, like the text it translates, is made up of individual words individually chosen, and every single word is problematic. One man's meat will continue to remain – and *should* continue to remain – another man's poison, and our three criteria, too, while providing us with a useful set of evaluative yardsticks, should certainly not be seen as offering any definitive and 'scientific' solution. There *is* no such final solution, whether to the evaluation of translations or interpretations or the sort of theoretical models we have been discussing here. Every reading, every interpretation, every translation, every theoretical model, every *narrating* is a particular strategy, a particular game, played with more or less accomplishment, but always according to its own particular rules. Some games, some models, are better for some purposes, for some people, than others are. Our evaluative criteria will always depend in the end on where we stand – and why we find ourselves standing there rather than somewhere else. 'Give me a place to stand, and I will move the world,' Archimedes is reported – in translation, of course – to have said. Recontextualized for the purposes of modern literary theory, the Archimedes Principle translates today as a reformulation of the Zeno Principle: 'Give me a place to read, and I will rewrite the world – subject only to the equal right of all other readers to do likewise.'

APPENDIX

A1   Es war an einem Sonntagvormittag im schönsten Frühjahr. Georg Bendemann, ein junger Kaufmann ... hatte gerade einen Brief an einen sich im Ausland befindenden Jugendfreund beendet [und] verschloss ihn in spielerischer Langsamkeit ... Er dachte darüber nach, wie dieser Freund, mit seinem Fortkommen zu Hause unzufrieden, vor Jahren schon nach Russland sich förmlich geflüchtet hatte ... Wie er erzählte, hatte er keine rechte Verbindung mit der dortigen Kolonie seiner Landsleute, aber auch fast keinen gesellschaftlichen Verkehr mit einheimischen Familien und richtete sich so für ein endgültiges Junggesellentum ein. (Kafka, 'Das Urteil' 8)

A2 It was a Sunday morning in the very height of spring. Georg
Bendemann, a young merchant ... had just finished a letter to an old
friend of his who was now living abroad [and] had put it into its
envelope in a slow and dreamy fashion ... He was thinking about
his friend, who had actually run away to Russia some years before,
being dissatisfied with his prospects at home ... By his own account
he had no regular connection with the colony of his fellow country-
men out there and almost no social intercourse with Russian families, so that he was resigning himself to becoming a permanent
bachelor. ('The Judgment,' trans. Muir and Muir, 49–50)

A3 It was a Sunday morning in the height of spring. Georg Bendemann,
a young businessman ... had just finished a letter to an old friend of
his who was now living abroad [and] toyed with it for a while as he
slowly sealed it ... He recalled how many years ago this friend of
his, dissatisfied with his progress at home, had quite simply decamped to Russia ... By his own account he had no real contact with
the colony of his fellow-countrymen out there, and indeed hardly
any social intercourse with Russian families, so that he was resigning himself to becoming a permanent bachelor. ('The Judgment,'
trans. Pasley, 1)

A4 It was a Sunday morning at the height of spring. George Bendemann,
a young businessman ... had just completed a letter to a boyhood
friend now living abroad [and] sealed it with frivolous deliberation
... He was thinking about how the friend, not content with his
progress at home, had years before quite literally escaped to Russia
... By his own account he had no proper contact with his compatri-
ots, who formed a colony in the city, and virtually no social intercourse with Russian families either, so that he was settling down to
a life of permanent bachelordom. ('The Judgement,' trans.
Underwood, 45)

A5 C'était un dimanche matin, dans la beauté du printemps. Georges
Bendemann, un jeune négociant ... venait d'achever une lettre à un
ami d'enfance résidant à l'étranger [et] l'avait fermée avec une
lenteur feinte ... Ses pensées suivaient cet ami qui, insatisfait de la

situation qu'on lui avait faite chez lui, s'était, quelques années auparavant, pour ainsi dire enfui en Russie ... D'après ses récits, non seulement il ne s'était guère lié avec ses compatriotes, mais il n'avait également aucune relation sociale avec les familles indigènes et, de cette façon, se vouait à un célibat définitif. ('Le jugement,' trans. Meylan, 9–13)

A6   C'était un matin de dimanche, par une année qui débutait splendidement. Georges Bendemann, un jeune négociant ... venait de terminer une lettre à un ami de jeunesse qui habitait l'étranger [et] commença par la fermer avec lenteur ... Il réfléchissait au destin de cet ami qui, mécontent de piétiner au pays, s'était littéralement enfui en Russie ... Il n'avait, a ce qu'il disait, aucune relation réelle avec la colonie de ses compatriotes, et presque aucun rapport non plus avec la société indigène; il semblait donc se préparer un célibat définitif. ('Le verdict,' trans. Vialatte, 41–2)

A7   Era una domenica mattina di primavera, faceva un tempo splendido. Il giovane commerciante Giorgio Bendemann ... aveva appena finito una lettera per un amico di gioventú che si trovava all'estero, la chiuse lentamente ... Pensava all'amico che, insoddisfatto per quanto gli offriva il suo paese, parecchi anni avanti era letteralmente fuggito in Russia ... Raccontava di non avere stretto rapporti con la colonia dei suoi compatrioti, mentre ben scarse erano le sue relazioni con la gente del posto; era ormai rassegnato a rimanere celibe. ('La condanna,' trans. Zampa, 99)

A8   Era una mattinata domenicale nel momento più bello della primavera. Giorgio Bendemann, un giovane commerciante ... aveva finito allora una lettera ad un amico d'infanzia che viveva all'estero; la chiuse con una lentezza compiaciuta, quasi giocherellando ... Meditava sul fatto che questo amico, scontento della sua esistenza in famiglia, già da anni s'era come rifugiato in Russia ... Secondo quel che raccontava non era in rapporti attivi colla colonia dei suoi connazionali, né aveva stretto quasi nessuna relazione d'amicizia con famiglie del luogo e s'avviava così a restar definitivamente scapolo. ('La condanna,' trans. Paoli, 141)

A9. Era una mañana de domingo, en plena primavera. Georg Bendemann, joven comerciante ... acababa de escribir una carta a un amigo de infancia que se encontraba en el extranjero [y] la cerró distraída y lánguidamente ... Pensaba en su amigo, que algunos años antes, disconforme con las perspectivas que su patria le ofrecía, se había ido a Rusia ... Según él decía, no tenía mayores relaciones con la colonia de compatriotas en aquella ciudad ni tampoco amistades entre las familias del lugar, de modo que su destino parecía ser una definitiva soltería. ('La condena,' trans. Wilcock, 9–10)

B1   In diesem Augenblick ging über die Brücke ein geradezu unendlicher Verkehr. (Kafka, 'Das Urteil,' 19)

B2   At this moment an unending stream of traffic was just going over the bridge. ('The Judgment,' trans. Muir and Muir, 63)

B3   At that moment the traffic was passing over the bridge in a positively unending stream. ('The Judgment,' trans. Pasley, 12)

B4   Crossing the bridge at that moment was a simply endless stream of traffic. ('The Judgement,' trans. Underwood, 56)

B5   En cet instant, il y avait justement sur le pont un trafic immense. ('Le jugement,' trans. Meylan, 63)

B6   A ce moment, il y avait sur le pont une circulation littéralement folle. ('Le verdict,' trans. Vialatte, 53)

B7   In quel momento il ponte era percorso da un traffico interminabile. ('La condanna,' trans. Zampa, 113)

B8   In quel momento sul ponte c'era un interminabile andirivieni di persone e di veicoli. ('La condanna,' trans. Paoli, 154)

B9   En ese momento una interminable fila de vehículos pasaba por el puente. ('La condena,' trans. Wilcock, 21)

Conclusion

Narrative, as portrayed by narratology, itself also a narrative, is in the end essentially an ironic and thus a ludic genre, an affair of message and metalinguistic commentary with each message and each commentary being relativized by the next higher levels in the narrative hierarchy. At the level of story, as I have written elsewhere (O'Neill 1990: 101–2), all is serious, all is real: 'This is so.' At the level of discourse the narrator essentially says, 'This is *not* so,' for by his or her employment of all the tricks of the narrative trade, flashbacks and flashforwards, permanent manipulation of order and duration, repetitions and omissions, focalization on or through this character instead of that one, and so on, the narrator essentially shows that on the level of discourse there is no one real or substantial story holding the entire narrative structure together, but only a series of events whose ultimate relevance is precisely their arrangeability. The narrator's discourse is in its turn relativized by the implied author, whose world is relativized by the empirical author, whose world is relativized by the web of intertextuality in which we all have our being, weaving our 'own' texts as they weave us.

Roman Jakobson famously observed that poetic language involved the projection of the vertical or paradigmatic axis of language onto the horizontal or syntagmatic axis (1960: 358). Narrative, as a structure of structures, rather involves the projection of the horizontal axis onto the vertical. Victor Shklovsky once defended *Tristram Shandy* against critics who complained of its formlessness as being 'the most typical novel in world literature' (1965: 57) in its privileging of discourse over story. By the same token it is also an archetypal literary example of the Zeno Principle, of narrative's tendency *not* to tell the story, a task the naïve reader might well think of as the entire *raison d'être* of the narrative in the first place, but rather to reflect on its own process of production. Tristram's narrative pace is so discursive – *sat verbum* – and his shaping of his own story so complicated that its completion becomes an impossibility, for 'the more I write the more I shall have to write' (230). While Sterne, like many other 'experimental' writers, achieves his literary and aesthetic effects by the conscious incorporation of discursive subversion, however, the result is in one sense merely to foreground an aspect of narrative that is always already in play, for ultimately all narratives, as Zeno demonstrated, necessarily actualize to a greater or lesser extent the theoretical potential for subversion inherent in their essentially ludic discursive structure.

Narrative and narratology are indissolubly linked, and that is certainly the best reason why a student of literary narrative also always needs to be a student of narratology. There is, of course, no reason at all why one should not study narrative theory primarily for its own sake, for 'pure' narrative theory is a wholly valid and independent discipline, and no apologies of any sort are needed in the final decade of the twentieth century for choosing to practise it. For those whose primary interest is literary rather than theoretical texts, however, 'applied' narratology, depending on how we choose to use it, can function either peripherally to our critical endeavours, as a mere mechanical handbook of occasionally useful technical terms, or centrally, as an indispensable and highly sophisticated model for generating more differentiated, more self-aware, more *interesting* readings. Ultimately, reading is what the study of literature is all about, and the better our reading is, the better in turn the texts we read will be. The play between story and discourse, narrative and narratology, practice and theory, reading and writing has emerged over recent decades as an inherent and inescapable factor in the way we see texts, and if the traditional reader's greatest ambition was precisely to stop reading, to reach a definitive and satisfactory conclusion to the work of reading and leave it at that, the post-modern reader's ambition is rather to continue reading, to prolong the game of reading and the play of story and discourse of which he or she too is a unique and vital factor.

Narrative theory in the tradition of formalist and structuralist narratology has two quite distinct faces, one belonging essentially to the sphere of work, the other belonging essentially to the sphere of play. In its earlier mode, that of Russian formalism and the scientific structuralism of the sixties, narratology functions essentially as a tool for finding serious-minded scientific answers, invariable rules, explanatory models that illustrate how narratives work. In its later, post-structuralist mode, flamboyantly introduced by Barthes's *S/Z* in 1970, narratology functions as a ludic rather than a scientific methodology for identifying (and multiplying) questions rather than answers, meanings rather than meaning, metaphors rather than truths, as structural analysis gives way to textual play, the search for origins becomes less important than the co-constructive role of readerly interpretation, and scientific rules revealing the truth about narrative become less important than ludic rules governing textual games.

Narratology in the nineties is still very much alive and well, but its once dominant position in international narrative theory has been powerfully challenged on an increasing variety of fronts by various versions of what one can most appropriately call post-narratological theories, *post-* in the double sense that they both come after and build upon the achievements of structuralist and post-structuralist narrative theory, though frequently to very different ends. In the systemic and still continuing reorganization of intellectual space that will undoubtedly emerge as the most enduring legacy of the theory boom of recent decades, narrative theory in its post-narratological phase has increasingly demonstrated an imperialist tendency to explode into a unified field theory of cultural studies in general, a Grand Universal Theory of Everything, as a glance at the program of any recent meeting of the Modern Language Association or the Society for the Study of Narrative Literature makes abundantly clear.

This development, in turn, while entirely valid in itself, has involved a large-scale turning away of the main line of academic interest in North America over the past decade from formalism in its various shapes, not only from the literary critical formalism of the Anglo-American New Criticism of the forties and fifties and the nuts-and-bolts structuralist formalism of a Greimas or the early Barthes of the sixties but also from the flamboyant neo-formalism of the post-structuralist deconstruction of the seventies, so rapidly and epidemically successful in North American academia that it equally rapidly grew itself to death over a span of little more than a decade. In place of any brand of formalism, multifarious versions and mutations of what has now come to be generally known as the New Historicism, a strongly politicized grouping of post-structuralist theoretical orientations drawing on a heterogeneous but highly potent mixture of sources, most notably neo-Marxism, Foucauldian discourse analysis, Derridean and de Manian deconstruction, Lacanian psychoanalysis, Bakhtinian dialogism, and a variety of feminisms, have seized centre stage in North American narrative theory (as in other branches of literary theory) during the eighties and nineties. Different though their individual critical concerns may be, these neo-historicist orientations tend to share a common conception of cultural discourse, one most fittingly emblematized in narratological terms by the grandly conceived overarching metanarrative constructs of a Lyotard, the individual subject seen as functioning always in the role of a character in a variety of simultaneous and intersecting metanarratives or grand narratives largely or wholly beyond our individual control, such as the narratives of history, race, nationality, and gender.[1]

In the course of this paradigmatic shift in emphasis in the development of narrative theory in general, interest in specifically literary narrative, even among specifically literary theorists, has lost very considerable ground to interest in cultural, ideological, and political narratives, as narrative theory in the newly expanded sense increasingly swallows up literary theory whole, while what was once literary theory increasingly becomes as part of the process cultural theory or critical theory or just plain theory *tout court*, progressively invading in the process the intellectual high ground once occupied by theology and later by philosophy. This post-narratological, post-structuralist, post-modern narrative theory, to put it another way, has become increasingly more contextualist and in the process increasingly critical of those contexts, as the implications of what Lyotard (1984: 27–31) has called the specifically *narrative* legitimation and authentication of social structures in a post-modern society become more evident.

It is worth remembering that this systemic shift of interest in mainstream narrative theory away from the concerns of narratology in the narrower sense by no means either replaces or discredits narratology as a discipline, however – any more than a growing interest in the game of tennis discredits the games of baseball or golf. Nor does it place these newer theoretical orientations beyond the reach of narratology as an explanatory (and exploratory) model. All of the new critical directions in narrative theory, however various their individual interests and however far those interests may have moved from the nuts and bolts of narrative structure in a narratological sense, focus specifically on narrative *discourse* and its multiple discursive possibilities, for narrative authority always means discursive authority. To put it in the specific terms of our narratological model as developed here: while realist critical concerns focused essentially on the level of story, and modernist critical concerns focused essentially on that of intratextual discourse, post-modernist critical concerns, whatever their specific area of emphasis, have increasingly come to focus on what we have here called the narrative level of textuality, extratextual discourse, that level for which the narratology of the sixties had no place in its conceptual repertoire. As the systemic importance of narrative as a theoretical tool of all work for cultural studies in general continues to grow, so, too, does the importance of continuing our investigation of narrative discourse itself, of rereading (and rewriting) the crucial and always mutually constitutive relationship, emblematically interrogated by Zeno, between the tale and its telling, story and discourse, narrative and narratology.

Notes

INTRODUCTION

1 The term *readerly* here and throughout is used as meaning 'pertaining to the reader' and is thus simply a convenient parallel for the term *authorial* 'pertaining to the author' – rather than contrasting 'readerly' and 'writerly' modes of reading as in Barthes's *S/Z* (1974).

CHAPTER 1

1 Succinct and accessible introductions to the intellectual tradition of formalism, structuralism, and semiotics, with valuable bibliographical references, are variously provided by Robert Scholes (1974), Jonathan Culler (1975), and Terence Hawkes (1977).
2 Of these, Rimmon-Kenan's excellent book, published in the New Accents series, is both the most accessible and the most systematic introduction to the field, while Gerald Prince's *A Dictionary of Narratology* (1989) is an invaluable work of reference. Both contain very useful bibliographies. For a comprehensive discussion of the range of twentieth-century theories of narrative, see Martin (1986). Other important recent general works include Cohan/Shires (1988), Genette (1988), Coste (1989), and Chatman (1990).
3 We shall return to this co-constructive role of the reader in chapter

5, in considering the role of textuality as a factor in narrative structure.

4 For general introductions to reader theory, see Suleiman/Crosman (1980) and also Tompkins (1980). For particularly useful studies, from a variety of theoretical positions, see Iser (1974), Pratt (1977), Eco (1979a), Fish (1980), Holub (1984), and Freund (1987).

5 Cf. Aristotle (1971: 51–2, 62); Chatman (1978: 19–20); Prince (1989: 49).

6 It is thus indicative that while the term *text* is entirely crucial for Rimmon-Kenan's (three-level) purposes, Prince, primarily a story-theorist, omits the term altogether in his excellent *Dictionary of Narratology* (1989).

7 On games and play in general, Huizinga (1949) and Caillois (1961) are classic texts, while Suits (1978) is a brilliant recent contribution. On specifically literary games and play, see Wilson (1990).

8 For a fuller discussion, see O'Neill (1990: 69–73), partly summarized here.

9 Hrushovski (1974: 21–2), quoted by Rimmon-Kenan (36).

CHAPTER 2

1 E.g., Booth (1961), Lubbock (1963), Forster (1979).

2 The epistolary novel can also provide interesting examples of pro-lepsis, again stressing the primacy of discourse over story. The real reader, for example, may be allowed to read a particular letter before its fictional recipient can do so – or even before it has been written by its fictional author.

3 All the more so since the 'defining' narrator may be internal or external, a point to which the next chapter will return.

4 *Existents* is Chatman's inclusive term for both characters and setting – as opposed to *events*, a term that includes both actions and happenings (1978: 19, 96).

5 The effect of this, it may be observed, can be very similar to the effect generated by our sense as readers as to where the *authorial* voice is coming from. Borges thematizes this in 'Pierre Menard, Author of the *Quixote*,' in which a French symbolist poet recreates certain passages of Cervantes' novel word for word: 'Cervantes'

text and Menard's are verbally identical, but the second is almost
infinitely richer' (*Labyrinths* 42).

CHAPTER 3

1 More finely calibrated intermediate stages of what is essentially
an infinitely variable scale could obviously be devised: Rimmon-
Kenan (1983: 109–10), following Brian McHale, identifies seven.
The three basic positions (maximally diegetic, mixed, maximally
mimetic) are variously named by various theorists: in traditional
usage they are usually called omniscient narration, free indirect
discourse (French *style indirect libre*, German *erlebte Rede*), and
interior monologue respectively; Genette (1980: 171–2) uses the
terms narratized, transposed, and immediate speech; Cohn (1978:
11–13) favours psycho-narration, narrated monologue, and quoted
monologue; and Rimmon-Kenan (109–10) prefers diegetic summary, indirect discourse, and direct discourse.
2 Chatman's claim that there are 'nonnarrated' stories (1978: 166) is
entirely untenable – as he himself later acknowledges (1990: 115).
There is *always* a narrator, who/which voices every word of the text
we read, including even those maximally mimetic situations where
characters produce apparently unmediated discourse (but whose
mediated nature is evident if only from the fact that as one element
in the overall narrative context it must always begin and end at
functionally significant rather than arbitrary points).
3 In Genette's typology, the key technical term *diegesis* (French
diégèse) means 'story' (Genette 1972: 72n; 1980: 27n). Confusingly
for English-speaking readers, the more established English usage,
as we saw in chapter 2, is that *diegesis* means 'telling, recounting
(French *diégésis*) as opposed to *mimesis* 'showing, enacting' (Prince
1989: 20), both of which clearly belong to the realm of *discourse*
rather than *story*. In English, of course, as we have also seen, the
terms *narrative, narration, story, account*, and *tale* offer exactly the
same possibility for confusion, in that they can all, in non-technical
usage, likewise mean either the product or the process of narration.
I follow Bal (1977) and Rimmon-Kenan (1983: 140n7) in using the
term *hypodiegetic* rather than Genette's *metadiegetic* (1980: 228n41),

though Genette himself, in a latter work, energetically rejects the proposed emendation (1988: 91–2).

4 For further discussion of the categorization of narrators in these terms, see Rimmon-Kenan (1983: 86–103).

5 The terms *external narrator* and *character-narrator* are based on Bal's usage, though her term *character-bound narrator*, applying only to narrators who appear as characters in their *own* narratives (1985: 122), has a more limited meaning than my term *character-narrator*.

6 In spite of the strong temptation to conceive of the narrative voice in a narrative written by a male author as being itself male, we need in principle to see a truly external narrator as unsexed. The more evidence there is of a gendered voice, the more the external narrator moves towards becoming a character-narrator.

7 Thus Booth (1961: 70–1), Chatman (1978: 147–51), and Chatman again (1990: 74–108).

8 In geometrical terms, a gnomon is the remainder of a parallelogram after the removal of a similar parallelogram containing one of its corners – and so called because of the resemblance of the resulting shape to a carpenter's square (Gk. *gnōmōn*). Serendipitously, Greek *gnōmōn* is literally 'one who knows, an interpreter,' cognate with Latin *gnārus* 'one who knows,' whence *narrator*.

9 Thus Genette (1980: 259–60), Rimmon-Kenan (1983: 89), and Bal (1985: 119–20) all exclude the implied author and implied reader; Chatman (1978: 150) sees both narrator and narratee as merely optional; Toolan (1988: 77) excludes the implied author and the implied reader and sees the narratee as merely optional. Conversely, however, other theorists have variously proposed the inclusion of several further narrative agents not considered here, such as the 'dramatized' author and narrator and the 'model' or 'virtual' reader. For further discussion and bibliographical references see Martin (1986: 152–72).

10 Wayne Booth sees his 'implied' author as an essentially anthropomorphic entity, 'the author's second self' (1961: 71), while Chatman's implied author is really an inferred author, a semiotically necessary but abstract construct put together by the reader as his concept of the author demanded by the text (1978: 148).

11 For an introduction to the operation of the actantial model in narrative, see Greimas (1983: 197–221); for a very brief summary see Rimmon-Kenan (1983: 34–6).

CHAPTER 4

1 It is indicative that the index of so authoritative a publication as Chatman's *Story and Discourse* (1978), which sets out to provide a comprehensive approach to a general theory of narrative, contains no entry for focalization.

2 Other terms have been suggested, e.g., 'orientation' (Toolan 1988: 68), or a combination of 'slant' and 'filter' (Chatman 1990: 143).

3 Theorists differ interestingly in the terms they use to describe the nature of the focalizer: Genette, who is primarily interested in focalization by *characters*, calls it the 'focal character' (1980: 188); Rimmon-Kenan calls it a 'vehicle' as well as an 'agent' (1983: 74, 78); Bal describes it as a 'point' or an 'agent' (1985: 104, 121); and Toolan usefully sees it as a 'refracting lens' (1988: 71).

4 Genette's conception of internal and external focalization (1980: 189), followed by Prince (1989: 31–3), differs from that of both Bal and Rimmon-Kenan: his 'internal' focalization is roughly the same as theirs; but his 'external' focalization actually refers less to the focalizer than to what I shall be calling a non-transparent *focalized* (Bal 1977: 28–9; qtd. Rimmon-Kenan 1983: 139n6). What I call external focalization, meanwhile (following Bal and Rimmon-Kenan), Genette prefers to call 'non-' or 'zero-focalized.' This, however, is quite unsatisfactory for the same reason as was Chatman's later decision to refer to 'non-narrated' narrative (1978: 166) – namely that *all* narrative is always both narrated *and* focalized.

5 Here I must disagree with Chatman, who, though he actually proposes the term *slant* to describe precisely this vision, argues that narrators and characters should properly not be regarded as focalizers in the same sense (1990: 145).

6 I owe the concept of primary and secondary focalization to Mieke Bal (1985: 112), whose usage also suggested the notational convention employed here.

7 The complexity of the focalization in this example is increased by the fact that the narrator-focalizer, Nelly Dean, is herself a hypo-diegetic narrator in the first-person narration of Mr Lockwood.

8 Rimmon-Kenan, like Bal, treats focalization as an element of text, but notes that there are also reasons for treating it rather as an element of narration (1993: 85).

9 Here I must disagree with Genette, who attributes such paratextual information to the narrator rather than the implied author (1988: 68n). Genette's attribution cannot, for example, adequately account for the titles of narratives with multiple sequential narrators, such as *The Sound and the Fury*.

CHAPTER 5

1 Cf. O'Neill (1990: 88–96, 109–27). I silently plagiarize my previous argument as necessary in the present chapter, 'considering self-plagiarism a legitimate activity,' as Rimmon-Kenan, on a similar occasion, elegantly puts it (1983: 137n3).

2 For recent developments in literary possible words theory, see Pavel (1986) and McHale (1987), also Doležel (1984).

3 The 'text' contained in my terms *intratextual* and *extratextual* always refers to the strictly limited concept of text propounded by narrato-logical theory, the concept with which we have been working so far. In the much extended sense current in post-structuralist usage the 'text' includes not only the words upon the page but also the textualizing activity of writing and reading those words. In this latter sense of 'text' the term *extratextual* would therefore be mean-ingless in the context of a literary discussion.

4 For a recent and excellent discussion of textuality as a factor in the reception of narrative as a discursive system, but without any attempt to incorporate such a discussion into the conceptual framework of classical narratology, see Cohan/Shires (1988: 1–51, 113–75). See also Martin (1986: 152–72).

5 The term *metatext* appears to have been coined by Anton Popovič (1976: 225). The term *intertextuality* was introduced by Julia Kristeva (1980: 66) in a discussion of Mikhail Bakhtin's related concept of textual dialogism (cf. Bakhtin 1981; Holquist 1990: 20–1, 88–9).

6 German formalist criticism during the 1940s, we may notice in

passing, likewise refers to itself as *werkimmanente Kritik* rather than *textimmanent*.

7 E.g., Pratt 1977; Suleiman/Crosman 1980; Tompkins 1980.

CHAPTER 6

1 Quoted by Susan Bassnett-McGuire (1980: 14), who provides an excellent introduction to the general field of translation studies.

2 For a collection of such aphorisms, see Koller 1987: 48–51.

3 Terry Eagleton (1983: 1–16) draws attention in exemplary fashion to the parallel relationship traditionally held to obtain between theory, criticism, and literature: the task of literary theory is to serve literary criticism, whose task in turn is to serve literature.

4 For such surveys, see Bassnett-McGuire (1980), Koller (1987); see also Lefevere (1982).

5 The reader need hardly be warned as to the highly dubious status of such neatly phrased summaries – this, after all, is only one of many such summaries I could have provided, and I am only one reader among many.

6 It should not be forgotten, of course, that I *find* particular effects striking in the first place because of my own overall reading of *Das Urteil*. Another reader might well ignore the effects I find most striking and focus instead on shadings that I ignore or have simply not been able to see.

7 It should also not be forgotten that I have no choice but to read all of the texts as a reader whose first language is and remains English. My ear for nuance and 'neutrality' will therefore clearly be quite different from that of a non-English speaker. This, however, is entirely in accordance with the assumptions of our third model.

8 The innocence of the 'literal' translation here, it need hardly be said, is also entirely questionable.

9 For further discussion of this reduced variant of the intertextual model, see Lefevere (1982: 148–9).

CONCLUSION

1 For a useful introduction to New Historicism, see Veeser (1989); see also Lodge (1990) and Fehn/Hoesterey/Tatar (1992).

Bibliography

This bibliography is made up of two separate listings, the first consisting of narrative and literary texts, the second of theoretical and critical texts. Items from the first list are cited in my own text by author and title. Items from the second list are referred to by author and date, where the date given is that of the edition cited rather than that of original publication (which latter is also noted in the bibliographical listing).

NARRATIVE AND LITERARY TEXTS

Anon. *The Arabian Nights*. Ed. Muhsin Mahdi. Trans. Husain Haddawy. New York, London: Norton, 1990.

Austen, Jane. *Northanger Abbey*. 1818. *The Collected Works of Jane Austen*. London: Octopus, 1980. 927–1052.

Balzac, Honoré de. *Père Goriot*. Orig. pub. as *Le père Goriot*, 1834. Trans. Henry Reed. New York: New American Library, 1962.

Barth, John. *Lost in the Funhouse: Fiction for Print, Tape, Live Voice*. 1968. New York: Bantam, 1981.

Beckett, Samuel. *Malone Dies*. Orig. pub. as *Malone meurt*, 1951. Trans. Samuel Beckett. *Three Novels by Samuel Beckett*. 177–288.

– *Molloy*. Orig. pub. in French, 1951. Trans. Patrick Bowles. *Three Novels by Samuel Beckett*. 5–176.

– *Three Novels by Samuel Beckett*. New York: Grove, 1965.

– *The Unnamable*. Orig. pub. as *L'innommable*, 1953. Trans. Samuel Beckett. *Three Novels by Samuel Beckett*. 289–414.

– *Watt*. 1953. New York: Grove; London: Evergreen, 1959.

Borges, Jorge Luis. *Labyrinths: Selected Stories and Other Writings*. Orig. pub. in Spanish, 1956–60. Trans. various. Ed. Donald A. Yates and James E. Irby. New York: New Directions, 1964.

Brontë, Emily. *Wuthering Heights*. 1847. Harmondsworth, UK: Penguin, 1961.

Calvino, Italo. *If on a Winter's Night a Traveler*. Orig. pub. as *Se una notte d'inverno un viaggiatore*, 1979. Trans. William Weaver. San Diego: Harvest-Harcourt, 1981.

Carroll, Lewis. *The Annotated Alice: Alice's Adventures in Wonderland and Through the Looking Glass*. Illus. John Tenniel. Intro. Martin Gardner. Forum Books. Cleveland, New York: World, 1970.

Cervantes Saavedra, Miguel de. *Don Quixote*. Orig. pub. as *El ingenioso hidalgo Don Quijote de la Mancha*, 1605–15. Trans. Peter Anthony Motteux. Intro. J.G. Lockhart. Everyman's Library. 2 vols. London: Dent, 1943.

Conrad, Joseph. *Heart of Darkness*. 1902. Ed. Robert Kimbrough. Norton Critical Edition. New York: Norton, 1963.

Cortázar, Julio. *Hopscotch*. Orig. pub. as *Rayuela*, 1963. Trans. Gregory Rabassa. 1966. New York: Bard-Avon, 1975.

Dickens, Charles. *Hard Times*. 1854. Signet Classics. New York: New American Library, 1964.

– *The Personal History of David Copperfield*. 1850. London: Gresham, n.d.

– *A Tale of Two Cities*. 1859. Signet Classics. New York: New American Library, 1980.

Döblin, Alfred. *Alexanderplatz, Berlin*. Orig. pub. as *Berlin Alexanderplatz*, 1929. Trans. Eugene Jolas. New York: Viking, 1931.

Dostoevsky, Feodor. *Crime and Punishment*. Orig. pub. in Russian, 1866. Trans. Jessie Coulson. Ed. George Gibian. Norton Critical Edition. New York: Norton, 1964.

Faulkner, William. *The Sound and the Fury*. 1929. Harmondsworth, UK: Penguin, 1965.

Flaubert, Gustave. *Madame Bovary*. Orig. pub. in French, 1857. Trans. Alan Russell. 1950. Harmondsworth, UK: Penguin, 1965.

Fontane, Theodor. *Effi Briest*. 1895. Frankfurt am Main: Insel, 1976.

Fowles, John. *The French Lieutenant's Woman*. 1969. Signet Classics. New York: New American Library, 1970.

- *The Magus*. 1965. New York: Dell, 1970.

García Márquez, Gabriel. *One Hundred Years of Solitude*. Orig. pub. as *Cien años de soledad*, 1967. Trans. Gregory Rabassa. New York: Bard-Avon, 1971.

George, Elizabeth. *A Great Deliverance*. New York: Bantam, 1988.

Goethe, Johann Wolfgang von. *Faust*. Orig. pub. in German, 1808–32. Trans. Bayard Taylor. 1870–1. London: Sphere, 1974.

Gogol, Nikolai Vasilevich. 'The Nose.' Orig. pub. in Russian, 1836. *Diary of a Madman and Other Stories*. Trans. Ronald Wilks. Harmondsworth, UK: Penguin, 1978.

Grass, Günter. *Cat and Mouse*. Orig. pub. as *Katz und Maus*, 1961. Trans. Ralph Manheim. 1963. New York: New American Library–Signet, 1964.

- *The Tin Drum*. Orig. pub. as *Die Blechtrommel*, 1959. Trans. Ralph Manheim. Vintage Books. New York: Random House, 1964.

Heller, Joseph. *Catch-22*. 1961. New York: Dell, 1962.

- *Something Happened*. 1974. New York: Ballantine, 1975.

Hesse, Hermann. *Steppenwolf*. Orig. pub. as *Der Steppenwolf*, 1927. Trans. Basil Creighton. Rev. Walter Sorrell. Harmondsworth, UK: Penguin, 1964.

Homer. *The Iliad of Homer*. Trans. Richmond Lattimore. 1951. Chicago, London: University of Chicago Press, 1961.

- *The Odyssey of Homer*. Trans. Richmond Lattimore. Perennial Library. New York: Harper & Row, 1975.

Joyce, James. *Dubliners*. 1914. Harmondsworth, UK: Penguin, 1961.

- *A Portrait of the Artist as a Young Man*. 1916. Harmondsworth, UK: Penguin, 1960.

- *Ulysses*. 1922. Ed. Hans Walter Gabler with Wolfhard Steppe and Claus Melchior. New York: Random House, 1986.

Kafka, Franz. 'La condanna.' *Racconti*. Trans. Giorgio Zampa. 1957. Milano: Feltrinelli, 1983.

- 'La condanna.' Trans. Rodolfo Paoli. *Racconti*. Ed. Ervino Pocar. 1970. Milano: Mondadori, 1980. 139–54.

- *La condena*. Trans. J.R. Wilcock. 1967. Buenos Aires: Alianza Editorial, 1978.

- 'The Judgment.' *The Penal Colony: Stories and Short Pieces*. Trans. Willa and Edwin Muir. 1948. New York: Schocken, 1970. 49–63.

- 'The Judgment.' Trans. Malcolm Pasley. *The Problem of The Judgment: Eleven Approaches to Kafka's Story*. Ed. Angel Flores. New York: Gordian Press, 1977. 1–12.
- 'The Judgement.' *Franz Kafka: Stories 1904–1924*. Trans. J.A. Underwood. London: Macdonald, 1981.
- *Le jugement*. Trans. Pierre Meylan. Porrentruy (Suisse): Editions des Portes de France, 1944.
- *The Metamorphosis*. Orig. pub. as *Die Verwandlung*, 1915. Trans. Willa and Edwin Muir. 1948. New York: Schocken, 1968.
- *Der Prozess*. 1925. Frankfurt am Main: Fischer Bücherei, 1964.
- *The Trial*. Orig. pub. as *Der Prozess*, 1925. Trans. Willa and Edwin Muir. 1937. New York: Schocken, 1968.
- 'Das Urteil.' 1913. *Franz Kafka: Das Urteil. Text, Materialien, Kommentar*, ed. Gerhard Neumann. München: Hanser, 1981. 7–19.
- 'Le verdict.' Trans. A. Vialatte. *Oeuvres complètes de Franz Kafka*. Ed. Marthe Robert. Paris: Gallimard, 1964. 4: 41–53.
Larson, Gary. *The Far Side*. Syndicated cartoon strip. Distributed by Universal Press Syndicate.
Le Carré, John. *A Small Town in Germany*. London: Pan, 1969.
Lewis, C.S. *The Complete Chronicles of Narnia*. 1950–6. 7 vols. Harmondsworth, UK: Penguin, 1979.
Lodge, David. *Nice Work*. 1988. Harmondsworth, UK: Penguin, 1989.
- *Small World: An Academic Romance*. 1984. Harmondsworth, UK: Penguin, 1985.
Macpherson, James. *The Poems of Ossian*. Leipzig: Tauchnitz, 1847.
Mann, Thomas. *Death in Venice*. Orig. pub. as *Der Tod in Venedig*, 1912. Trans. H.T. Lowe-Porter. 1928. Harmondsworth, UK: Penguin, 1971.
- *The Magic Mountain*. Orig. pub. as *Der Zauberberg*, 1924. Trans. H.T. Lowe-Porter. 1927. Harmondsworth, UK: Penguin, 1960.
Nabokov, Vladimir. *Lolita*. 1955. New York: Berkley, 1970.
- *Pnin*. 1957. Harmondsworth, UK: Penguin, 1960.
O'Brien, Flann (Brian O'Nolan). *At Swim-Two-Birds*. 1939. London: MacGibbon and Kee, 1966.
- *The Third Policeman*. 1967. London: Hart-Davis, MacGibbon, 1973.
Passant, E.J., with W.O. Henderson, C.J. Child, and D.C. Watt. *A Short History of Germany 1815–1945*. 1959. Cambridge: Cambridge University Press, 1962.

Pope, Alexander. *Poems*. Ed. John Butt. 11 vols. London: Methuen;
New Haven, CT: Yale University Press, 1939–69.

Potter, Beatrix. *The Tale of Jemima Puddleduck*. 1908. Harmondsworth,
UK: Frederick Warne-Penguin, 1986.

Proust, Marcel. *Remembrance of Things Past*. Orig. pub. as *A la recherche
du temps perdu*, 1913–27. Trans. C.K. Scott Moncrieff and Terence
Kilmartin; and (part 8) Andreas Mayor. 8 parts in 3 vols. New York:
Random House, 1981.

Pynchon, Thomas. *The Crying of Lot 49*. 1965. New York: Bantam, 1967.

Queneau, Raymond. *Exercises in Style*. Orig. pub. as *Exercices de style*,
1947. Trans. Barbara Wright. London: Gaberbocchus, 1958.

Rieu, E.V., trans. *The Four Gospels*. Harmondsworth, UK: Penguin, 1952.

Robbe-Grillet, Alain. *La Maison de Rendez-vous*. Orig. pub. as *La maison
de rendez-vous*, 1965. Trans. Richard Howard. 1966. New York: Grove,
1967.

– *The Voyeur*. Orig. pub. as *Le voyeur*, 1955. Trans. Richard Howard.
1958. New York: Grove, 1966.

Rushdie, Salman. *Midnight's Children*. 1981. London: Pan-Picador,
1982.

Shakespeare, William. *The Complete Works of William Shakespeare*.
Ed. W.J. Craig. London: Oxford University Press, 1962.

Stendhal (Marie-Henri Beyle). *Scarlet and Black*. Orig. pub. as *Le rouge et
le noir*, 1831. Trans. Margaret R.B. Shaw. 1953. Harmondsworth, UK:
Penguin, 1964.

Sterne, Laurence. *Tristram Shandy*. 1760–7. New York: Signet, 1960.

Stevenson, Robert Louis. *Kidnapped*. 1886. New York: Magnum, 1967.

Thackeray, William Makepeace. *Vanity Fair: A Novel without a Hero*.
1848. New York: New American Library, 1962.

Tolstoy, Leo. *Anna Karenina*. Orig. pub. in Russian, 1878. Trans. Louise
and Aylmer Maude. Ed. George Gibian. Norton Critical Edition.
New York: Norton, 1970.

– *War and Peace*. Orig. pub. in Russian, 1868–9. Trans. Ann Dunnigan.
New York: New American Library, 1968.

Virgil. *The Aeneid*. Trans. Robert Fitzgerald. Vintage Books. New York:
Random House, 1984.

Visconti, Luchino, director. *Death in Venice*. Film. With Dirk Bogarde.
Warner Brothers, 1971.

174 Bibliography

Voltaire (François-Marie Arouet). *Candide*. Orig. pub. in French, 1758. Trans. anon. Intro. Philip Littell. New York: Modern Library, 1950.

Watterson, Ben. *Calvin and Hobbes*. Syndicated cartoon strip. Distributed by Universal Press Syndicate.

THEORETICAL AND CRITICAL TEXTS

Aristotle. 1971. 'Poetics.' Trans. S.H. Butcher. 1955. *Critical Theory since Plato*. Ed. Hazard Adams. San Diego: Harcourt Brace Jovanovich. 47–66.

Armstrong, Paul B. 1983. 'The Conflict of Interpretations and the Limits of Pluralism.' *PMLA* 98 (1983): 341–52.

Bakhtin, M.M. 1981. *The Dialogic Imagination: Four Essays*. Orig. pub. in Russian, 1975. Ed. Michael Holquist. Trans. Caryl Emerson and Michael Holquist. Austin: University of Texas Press.

Bal, Mieke. 1977. *Narratologie. Essais sur la signification narrative dans quatre romans modernes*. Paris: Klincksieck.

– 1985. *Narratology: Introduction to the Theory of Narrative*. Orig. pub. in Dutch, 1980. Trans. Christine van Boheemen. Toronto: University of Toronto Press.

Baldick, Chris. 1990. *The Concise Oxford Dictionary of Literary Terms*. Oxford, New York: Oxford University Press.

Barthes, Roland. 1968. *Elements of Semiology*. Orig. pub. as *Eléments de sémiologie*, 1964. Trans. Annette Lavers and Colin Smith. New York: Hill and Wang.

– 1974. *S/Z*. Orig. pub. in French, 1970. Trans. Richard Miller. New York: Hill and Wang.

– 1977. *Image–Music–Text*. Essays selected and trans. Stephen Heath. New York: Hill and Wang.

– 1988. *The Semiotic Challenge*. Orig. pub. as *L'aventure sémiologique*, 1985. Trans. Richard Howard. New York: Hill and Wang.

Bassnett-McGuire, Susan. 1980. *Translation Studies*. New Accents. London, New York: Methuen.

Booth, Wayne C. 1961. *The Rhetoric of Fiction*. Chicago: University of Chicago Press.

Bremond, Claude. 1973. *Logique du récit*. Paris: Seuil.

Brooks, Cleanth, and Robert Penn Warren. 1959. *Understanding Fiction.* 1943. New York: Appleton-Century-Crofts.

Caillois, Roger. 1961. *Man, Play and Games.* Orig. pub. as *Les jeux et les hommes,* 1958. Trans. Meyer Barash. New York: Free Press of Glencoe.

Chatman, Seymour. 1978. *Story and Discourse: Narrative Structure in Fiction and Film.* Ithaca, NY and London: Cornell University Press.

– 1990. *Coming to Terms: The Rhetoric of Narrative in Fiction and Film.* Ithaca, NY and London: Cornell University Press.

Cohan, Steven, and Linda M. Shires. 1988. *Telling Stories: A Theoretical Analysis of Narrative Fiction.* New Accents. New York, London: Routledge.

Cohn, Dorrit. 1978. *Transparent Minds: Narrative Modes for Presenting Consciousness in Fiction.* Princeton, NJ: Princeton University Press.

Coste, Didier. 1989. *Narrative as Communication.* Foreword by Wlad Godzich. Theory and History of Literature 64. Minneapolis: University of Minnesota Press.

Culler, Jonathan. 1975. *Structuralist Poetics: Structuralism, Linguistics and the Study of Literature.* London: Routledge and Kegan Paul.

– 1981. *The Pursuit of Signs: Semiotics, Literature, Deconstruction.* Ithaca, NY: Cornell University Press.

de Man, Paul. 1983. *Blindness and Insight: Essays in the Rhetoric of Contemporary Criticism.* Theory and History of Literature 7. Minneapolis: University of Minnesota Press.

Derrida, Jacques. 1976. *Of Grammatology.* Orig. pub. as *De la grammatologie,* 1967. Trans. Gayatri Chakravorty Spivak. Baltimore, MD: Johns Hopkins University Press.

Doležel, Lubomír. 1984. 'Kafka's Fictional World.' *Canadian Review of Comparative Literature* 11 (1984): 61–83.

Durant, Alan, and Nigel Fabb. 1990. *Literary Studies in Action.* London: Routledge.

Eagleton, Terry. 1983. *Literary Theory: An Introduction.* Minneapolis: University of Minnesota Press.

Eco, Umberto. 1979. *A Theory of Semiotics.* Bloomington: Indiana University Press.

– 1979a. *The Role of the Reader: Explorations in the Semiotics of Texts.* Bloomington: Indiana University Press.

Erlich, Victor. 1981. *Russian Formalism: History – Doctrine.* 1955. New Haven, CT: Yale University Press.

Fehn, Ann, Ingeborg Hoesterey, and Maria Tatar. 1992. *Neverending Stories: Toward a Critical Narratology.* Princeton, NJ: Princeton University Press.

Fish, Stanley. 1980. *Is There a Text in This Class? The Authority of Interpretive Communities.* Cambridge, MA: Harvard University Press.

Forster, E.M. 1979. *Aspects of the Novel.* 1927. Ed. Oliver Stallybrass. Harmondsworth, UK: Penguin.

Frenz, Horst. 1973. 'The Art of Translation.' *Comparative Literature: Method and Perspective.* Ed. Newton P. Stallknecht and Horst Frenz. 1961. Carbondale: Southern Illinois University Press. 98–121.

Freund, Elizabeth. 1987. *The Return of the Reader: Reader-Response Criticism.* New Accents. London: Methuen.

Frye, Northrop. 1957. *Anatomy of Criticism: Four Essays.* Princeton, NJ: Princeton University Press.

Genette, Gérard. 1972. *Figures III.* Paris: Editions du Seuil.

– 1980. *Narrative Discourse: An Essay in Method.* Orig. pub. as 'Discours du récit' in *Figures III,* 1972. Trans. Jane E. Lewin. Ithaca, NY: Cornell University Press.

– 1988. *Narrative Discourse Revisited.* Orig. pub. as *Nouveau discours du récit,* 1983. Trans. Jane E. Lewin. Ithaca, NY: Cornell University Press.

Greimas, Algirdas Julien. 1983. *Structural Semantics: An Attempt at a Method.* Orig. pub. as *Sémantique structurale: Recherche de méthode,* 1966. Trans. Daniele McDowell, Ronald Schleifer, and Alan Velie. Lincoln, London: University of Nebraska Press.

Hawkes, Terence. 1977. *Structuralism and Semiotics.* Berkeley: University of California Press.

Holquist, Michael. 1990. *Dialogism: Bakhtin and His World.* New Accents. London: Routledge.

Holub, Robert C. 1984. *Reception Theory: A Critical Introduction.* New Accents. London: Methuen.

Hrushovski, Benjamin, and Ziva Ben-Porat. 1974. *Structuralist Poetics in Israel.* Tel Aviv: Porter Institute for Poetics and Semiotics.

Huizinga, Johan. 1949. *Homo Ludens: A Study of the Play Element in*

Culture. Orig. pub. in Dutch, 1938. Trans. R.F.C. Hull. London: Routledge.

Hutcheon, Linda. 1988. *A Poetics of Postmodernism: History, Theory, Fiction.* New York: Routledge.

Hutchinson, Peter. 1983. *Games Authors Play.* London: Methuen.

Iser, Wolfgang. 1971. 'The Reading Process: A Phenomenological Approach.' *New Literary History* 3 (1971): 279–99.

– 1974. *The Implied Reader: Patterns of Communication in Prose Fiction from Bunyan to Beckett.* Baltimore, MD: Johns Hopkins University Press.

Jakobson, Roman. 1956. 'Two Aspects of Language and Two Types of Aphasic Disturbances.' *Fundamentals of Language.* By Roman Jakobson and Morris Halle. The Hague: Mouton. 69–96.

– 1959. 'On Linguistic Aspects of Translation.' *On Translation.* Ed. R.A. Brower. Cambridge, MA: Harvard University Press.

– 1960. 'Closing Statement: Linguistics and Poetics.' *Style in Language.* Ed. Thomas A. Sebeok. Cambridge, MA: MIT Press. 350–77.

Jameson, Fredric. 1974. *The Prison-House of Language: A Critical Account of Structuralism and Russian Formalism.* 1972. Princeton, NJ: Princeton University Press.

– 1981. *The Political Unconscious: Narrative as a Socially Symbolic Act.* Ithaca, NY: Cornell University Press.

Kahrmann, Cordula, Gunter Reiss, and Manfred Schluchter. 1986. *Erzähltextanalyse: Eine Einführung mit Studien- und Übungstexten.* 1977. Königstein (Ts.): Athenäum.

Kanzog, Klaus. 1976. *Erzählstrategie: Eine Einführung in die Normeinübung des Erzählens.* Uni-Taschenbücher 495. Heidelberg: Quelle & Meyer.

Kayser, Wolfgang. 1954. *Entstehung und Krise des modernen Romans.* Stuttgart: Metzler.

Koller, Werner. 1987. *Einführung in die Übersetzungswissenschaft.* Uni-Taschenbücher 819. 1983. Heidelberg, Wiesbaden: Quelle & Meyer.

Kristeva, Julia. 1980. *Desire in Language: A Semiotic Approach to Literature and Art.* Orig. pub. in French, 1969–77. Ed. Leon S. Roudiez. Trans. Thomas Gora, Alice Jardine, and Leon S. Roudiez. New York: Columbia University Press.

Lämmert, Eberhart. 1955. *Bauformen des Erzählens*. Stuttgart: Metzler.

Lefevere, André. 1982. 'Théorie littéraire et littérature traduite.' *Canadian Review of Comparative Literature* 9 (1982): 137–56.

Leibniz, Gottfried Wilhelm. 1952. *Theodicy*. Orig. pub. as *Essais de théodicée sur la bonté de Dieu, la liberté de l'homme et l'origine du mal*, 1710. Ed. Austin Farrar. Trans. E.M. Huggard. London: Routledge.

Lentricchia, Frank. 1980. *After the New Criticism*. Chicago: University of Chicago Press.

Lévi-Strauss, Claude. 1963. *Structural Anthropology*. Orig. pub. as *Anthropologie structurale*, 1958. Trans. Claire Jacobson and Brooke Grundfest Schoepf. New York: Basic.

Lodge, David. 1990. *After Bakhtin: Essays on Fiction and Criticism*. London: Routledge.

Lotman, Jurij. 1977. *The Structure of the Artistic Text*. Orig. pub. in Russian, 1970. Trans. Ronald Vroon. Michigan Slavic Contributions 7. Ann Arbor: University of Michigan Press.

Lubbock, Percy. 1963. *The Craft of Fiction*. 1921. New York: Viking Press.

Lyons, John. 1977. *Semantics*. Cambridge: Cambridge University Press.

Lyotard, Jean-François. 1984. *The Postmodern Condition: A Report on Knowledge*. Orig. pub. as *La condition postmoderne: Rapport sur le savoir*, 1979. Trans. Geoff Bennington and Brian Massumi. Theory and History of Literature 10. Minneapolis: University of Minnesota Press.

McHale, Brian. 1987. *Postmodernist Fiction*. New York: Methuen.

Martin, Wallace. 1986. *Recent Theories of Narrative*. Ithaca, NY: Cornell University Press.

Miller, J. Hillis. 1990. 'Narrative.' *Critical Terms for Literary Study*. Ed. Frank Lentricchia and Thomas McLaughlin. Chicago: University of Chicago Press. 66–79.

Neumann, Gerhard. 1981. *Franz Kafka: Das Urteil. Text, Materialien, Kommentar*. München: Hanser.

O'Neill, Patrick. 1990. *The Comedy of Entropy: Humour, Narrative, Reading*. Toronto: University of Toronto Press.

Pavel, Thomas G. 1986. *Fictional Worlds*. Cambridge, MA: Harvard University Press.

Popovič, Anton. 1976. 'Aspects of Metatext.' *Canadian Review of Comparative Literature* 3 (1976): 225–35.

Pratt, Mary Louise. 1977. *Toward a Speech Act Theory of Literary Discourse*. Bloomington: Indiana University Press.

Prince, Gerald. 1971. 'Notes toward a Categorization of Fictional "Narratees."' *Genre* 4 (1971): 100–6.

– 1973. *A Grammar of Stories: An Introduction*. The Hague: Mouton.

– 1982. *Narratology: The Form and Functioning of Narrative*. Berlin: Mouton.

– 1989. *A Dictionary of Narratology*. 1987. Lincoln, London: University of Nebraska Press.

Propp, Vladimir. 1968. *Morphology of the Folktale*. Orig. pub. in Russian, 1928. Trans. Laurence Scott. Ed. Louis A. Wagner. Austin: University of Texas Press.

Rimmon-Kenan, Shlomith. 1983. *Narrative Fiction: Contemporary Poetics*. New Accents. London: Methuen.

Saussure, Ferdinand de. 1966. *Course in General Linguistics*. Orig. pub. as *Cours de linguistique générale*, 1915. Ed. Charles Bally and Albert Sechehaye, in collab. with Albert Riedlinger. Trans. Wade Baskin. 1959. New York: McGraw-Hill.

Scholes, Robert. 1974. *Structuralism in Literature: An Introduction*. New Haven, CT and London: Yale University Press.

Shklovsky, Victor. 1965. 'Sterne's *Tristram Shandy*: Stylistic Commentary.' Orig. pub. in Russian, 1921. *Russian Formalist Criticism: Four Essays*. Trans. Lee T. Lemon and Marion J. Reis. Lincoln, London: University of Nebraska Press. 25–57.

Souriau, Etienne. 1950. *Les deux cent mille situations dramatiques*. Paris: Flammarion.

Stanzel, F.K. 1955. *Die typischen Erzählsituationen im Roman*. Vienna: Braumüller.

– 1986. *A Theory of Narrative*. Orig. pub. as *Theorie des Erzählens*, 1979. Trans. Charlotte Goedsche. 1984. Cambridge: Cambridge University Press.

Suits, Bernard. 1978. *The Grasshopper: Games, Life and Utopia*. Toronto: University of Toronto Press.

Suleiman, Susan R., and Inge Crosman, eds. 1980. *The Reader in the Text: Essays on Audience and Interpretation*. Princeton, NJ: Princeton University Press.

180   Bibliography

Todorov, Tzvetan. 1966. 'Les catégories du récit littéraire.' *Communications* (Paris) 8 (1966): 125–51.
- 1969. *Grammaire du Décaméron.* The Hague: Mouton.
- 1977. *The Poetics of Prose.* Orig. pub. as *La poétique de la prose*, 1971. Trans. Richard Howard. Ithaca, NY: Cornell University Press.
- 1981. *Introduction to Poetics.* Orig. pub. in French, 1968. Trans. Richard Howard. Theory and History of Literature 1. Minneapolis: University of Minnesota Press.
Tompkins, Jane P., ed. 1980. *Reader-Response Criticism: From Formalism to Post-Structuralism.* Baltimore, MD: Johns Hopkins University Press.
Toolan, Michael J. 1988. *Narrative: A Critical Linguistic Introduction.* London: Routledge.
Veeser, H. Aram, ed. 1989. *The New Historicism.* New York: Routledge.
Wellek, René, and Austin Warren. 1962. *Theory of Literature.* 1942. New York: Harcourt Brace.
Wilson, R. Rawdon. 1990. *In Palamedes' Shadow: Explorations in Play, Game, and Narrative Theory.* Boston, MA: Northeastern University Press.

Index

86, 163; intradiegetic, 60, 72, 78; multiple, 64–5; omniscient, 46, 62; unreliable, 61, 63–4, 66, 67, 78
New Criticism, 69, 123, 139, 158
New Historicism, 158, 167
novel, 12, 156; epistolary, 162

O'Brien, Flann (Brian O'Nolan): *At Swim-Two-Birds*, 115, 124; *The Third Policeman*, 48
O'Neill, Patrick, 23, 125, 155, 162, 166
opera, 134, 135
Ossian, 137

paradox, 4–7, 31, 108, 110, 128, 129–30, 131, 149
parody, 69–70, 148
Passant, E.J., 105
Pavel, Thomas, 166
place, 33, 47–9, 53–4, 68
play, 4, 107, 162; and discourse, 108, 112, 113; and post-structuralism, 157; and textuality, 10, 27–8, 121, 129
poetry, 12
Pope, Alexander, 137; *The Rape of the Lock*, 137
Popovič, Anton, 166
possible worlds, 110–11. *See also* worlds, narrative
post-modernism, 4, 70, 124–5, 138, 157, 159
post-structuralism, 75, 82, 107, 158; and textuality, 116–17, 121–9 passim, 140, 141, 148, 166

Potter, Beatrix, 37, 102
Pratt, Mary Louise, 126, 162, 167
Prince, Gerald, 13, 76, 79, 161, 162; on narratee, 72; terminology, 17–18, 21, 163
prolepsis, 42, 43, 45–7, 115
Propp, Vladimir, 17
Proust, Marcel, 54; *Remembrance of Things Past*, 44
Pynchon, Thomas: *The Crying of Lot 49*, 52

Queneau, Raymond: *Exercises in Style*, 56–7

reader, 14–16, 49, 62, 71; and focalization, 100, 104; and textuality, 121, 125–7, 129–30; and translation, 139, 140, 141, 151; formalist, 70; implied, 71, 73–5, 77–8, 96, 109–10, 114, 130; manipulation of, 46, 81, 96; naïve, 22, 156; pre-formalist, 25, 69, 70, 157; real (versus implied), 72, 73–8 passim, 109–10, 114, 117, 130. *See also* reader theory; reading
reader theory, 25, 120, 121–3, 126, 129–30
reading, 8, 9, 66, 73–4, 87, 118, 120, 156; and writing, 9, 16, 18, 82, 119–20, 135, 156–7; as palimpsest, 127; historical paradigms of, 122–3; models of, 137, 139, 140, 148, 149. *See also* contextuality; reader; reader theory

realism, 37, 44, 122, 134, 159
relevance, narrative, 103–4, 133
reliability, narrative, 63–4, 66–7, 70; validation of, 68
Rieu, E.V., 94
Rimmon-Kenan, Shlomith, 13, 29, 130, 161–6 passim; on characterization, 50, 52; on focalization, 84, 86, 88, 92, 96; on implied author, 67; on narrative levels, 108; on time, 44; terminology, 17, 19–24 passim, 40
Robbe-Grillet, Alain: *La Maison de Rendez-vous*, 70, 125; *The Voyeur*, 48, 103–4
Rushdie, Salman: *Midnight's Children*, 37

Saussure, Ferdinand de, 30, 32
scene, 43
Scholes, Robert, 161
semantics, 111, 112, 128
semiotics, 13, 130, 138, 161; narrative as semiotic structure, 107, 109; semiotic criticism, 122, 128
setting, 8, 44, 47–9, 53–5, 68; discourse, 55–6
Shakespeare, William: *Hamlet*, 50, 134–5; *King Lear*, 48
Shklovsky, Victor, 20, 21, 155
Souriau, Etienne, 26
speech act theory, 126
Stanzel, Franz K., 83
Stendhal (Marie-Henri Beyle): *Scarlet and Black*, 44
Sterne, Laurence: *Tristram Shandy*, 135, 155–6

Stevenson, Robert Louis: *Kidnapped*, 47, 63
story, 3, 23, 24, 33–41 passim, 108, 155; and discourse, 3–9 passim, 20, 31, 33–57 passim, 131, 156; story-world, 40–1, 135
structuralism, 138, 140, 157, 161; French, 13
structure, narrative, 13, 42, 76, 107, 131, 155
subversion, narrative, 3–9 passim, 31, 83, 106, 108, 131, 156
Suits, Bernard, 27, 28, 125, 162
Suleiman, Susan R., and Inge Crosman, 162, 167
summary, 43
syntax, 112

terminology, 8–9, 20–2, 30, 69, 83, 85, 165, 166
text: autotelic, 139; narratological, 20–6 passim, 40, 95–6; post-structuralist, 107, 116, 117, 118, 166
textology, 107, 116, 120, 121, 123, 129
textuality, 23–5, 96, 107, 110, 116–31, 139, 141, 159, 162, 166. *See also* contextuality; extratextuality; intertextuality; intratextuality; metatextuality; text
Thackeray, William Makepeace, 52; *Vanity Fair*, 84–5, 86, 87
theory, 21–2, 151, 158–60, 167; as game, 26–32; narrative, 12–13, 29, 157, 158–60; post-structuralist, 27, 110, 126–7; translation, 138